MARKETPLACE
DIGNITY

CAIT LAMBERTON, NEELA A. SALDANHA, AND TOM WEIN

MARKETPLACE
DIGNITY

TRANSFORMING HOW WE ENGAGE *with* CUSTOMERS ACROSS THEIR JOURNEY

WHARTON SCHOOL PRESS

Published by
Wharton School Press
An Imprint of University of Pennsylvania Press
Philadelphia, Pennsylvania 19104–4112
wsp.wharton.upenn.edu

Printed in the United States of America on acid-free paper

10 9 8 7 6 5 4 3 2 1

Ebook ISBN: 9781613631768
Paperback ISBN: 9781613631744
Institutional Hardcover ISBN: 9781613631751

Contents

Introduction

Why do your customers behave the way they do? What makes them engage or disengage with your brand, products, and services?

Your product might be the most refreshing soda or the most nutritious breakfast oats on the market. Your store might boast the widest selection of goods or the most useful staff expertise in the neighborhood. Your organization might offer the best remedy to a social problem. But there's still no guarantee that your customers will buy what you have to offer.

Marketers have sought to unlock the mysteries of human behavior since human beings first began trading with one another. Over the centuries, a number of theories have taken hold about why we make choices and the ideas and feelings that compel us to buy one product, choose one service, or engage with one brand or organization over another. Many of the theories are rooted in ideas from antiquity.

For Plato, grappling with the intricacies of the human psyche in the third century BC, behavior could be understood in terms of three distinct elements or levers: *reason, appetite,* and *spirit.*

Reason is the cognitive element of our psyche, manifest in the deliberate way we process information and make choices based on data. Appetite, the intuitive or affective element, relates to the more impulsive, emotional drivers in decision-making. If these two systems sound familiar to you, it's because over time, we (behavioral

1

economists, professors and students of marketing, researchers, and society in general) have largely come to understand human trade (and capitalism itself) in terms of this dual system: mind versus body, head versus heart, logic versus emotion, systematic versus heuristic— we've kind of agreed that human behavior can be distilled into a dualism of reason and appetite. Further, over time, we've gotten busy organizing the way we market our goods and services according to this dual system, optimizing our efforts to appeal to rational and careful purchasing, as well as the notorious impulse buy. We market for reason and appetite. But what about Plato's third lever? What about spirit?

Consider this anecdote. Back in 2010, as a young mother, Neela took her iPhone to the store to have it fixed. Her phone's speaker was jammed with baby food. When she got to the head of the line and explained the problem, the customer service representative listened politely for a brief moment and told her that she could probably remove the baby food with a safety pin or something similar. He sent her home. But here's the thing: this same representative had spent several minutes laughing and patiently helping the customer ahead of Neela, a customer who seemed like he wanted his entire home wired. Neela felt her experience was materially different from the customer ahead of her. The customer service representative did not try to engage her in a similar manner as the person in front of her, and he dismissed her concern. Neela couldn't explain why she felt bad (after all, it was a funny story, and she told it at many dinner parties!), but she vowed never to buy a phone from the same company again. Fourteen years later, she still hasn't.

What went wrong here? Neela's anecdote illustrates what happens when firms optimize for reason and appetite but fail to respect the third dimension of customers' behavioral and decision-making levers: their dignity.

What Plato calls our human *spirit* is our need to be seen and heard, to feel that we have agency in or control over our interactions and transactions, and to be treated equitably and fairly. Neela's customer service representative was not rude. But in dismissing her small problem, this employee unwittingly lost her business. While it is reasonable to treat customers in different ways based on their loyalty and engagement with an organization, each customer wants to be treated with a minimum of respect and care. Among other things, that means valuing their time.

Neela's is a small, everyday anecdote. But it probably resonates with you or someone you know. In this book, we will share a range of examples, big and small, corporate and personal, of what happens when firms do not prioritize their customers' dignity; we call this a failure to acknowledge *marketplace dignity*. And we're going to explore what you and your brand stand to gain when you design for marketplace dignity and how you go about doing so.

First, let's look at what we mean by dignity: how it manifests and why it is so important.

Dignity: What It Isn't, What It Is, and Why It Matters

In 1948, as the world was reeling from the atrocities committed during World War II, the United Nations (UN) issued a statement—an assertion—about our complex, shared humanity. And they enshrined this declaration into international law with the goal of helping maintain equilibrium, peace, and prosperity for all:

> All human beings are born free and equal in dignity and rights. They are endowed with reason and conscience and should act toward one another in a spirit of brotherhood.[1]

The UN Universal Declaration of Human Rights provides a useful benchmark for thinking about dignity as something inalienable; something that is fundamental and inherent to every human being; something demanding that we each be treated in a certain, specific way and with a certain consideration.

But what *is* dignity? And how does dignity manifest in individuals and in our behavior? In trying to define dignity, it is easier in some ways to say what it isn't first, rather than what it is.

Let's look at three human attributes that are sometimes mistaken for dignity but that are not quite the same thing.

Dignity Is Not Self-Esteem

Self-esteem comes from within but is strongly influenced by the environment in which we interact, achieve, and experience feedback. As such, self-esteem is variable, and it is contingent—it can be increased through achievement and a sense of accomplishment. In this sense, it is tied to our own actions. Dignity, on the other hand, is something inherent, and it is essentially stable—you have it no matter what. Unlike self-esteem, dignity cannot increase or decrease. But dignity is affirmed or offended against by other people. Whether our dignity is affirmed or denied may affect self-esteem, but lacking self-esteem does not mean that one has less inherent dignity.

Dignity Is Not Pride

Pride is an emotion we feel when we have achieved something or attained a certain status. When we become proud, we are focused on being given credit for what we've done and showing it to other people. There can then be danger here. Other people can question our right to claim credit. Or we might fail to continue achieving in the same way, and by doing so, experience the proverbial fall. Dignity, by contrast, is about *who we are* as humans, not *what we achieve or do*.

Dignity Is Not Status or Identity

Dignity doesn't default to one set of people over another. It isn't the same as status. When we are underrepresented or misrepresented in any context, that denies our dignity. However, even when we don't have a voice, we can still exercise personal agency to push back and reclaim our dignity to some extent. But it's hard. The world is full of systems and norms, as well as societal structures and experiences that represent some more than others. And in this sense, the affirmation or denial of dignity is again contingent on the way other people treat us in the external world.

There are really two key ideas that emerge by talking about what dignity isn't. The first is that dignity is about identity, not actions—an identity that all of us share as humans. The second is that dignity is about the way other people see and treat us. In this sense, we can define having dignity as being valued and respected *by other people* not for what we do, but for *who we are*.

Let's turn that around for you in terms of your organization and your customers. Treating your customers with dignity means showing every customer that you value and respect them because of who they are, regardless of what they buy from you or how they engage with your brand.

Above all, every customer should be treated in a way that respects their inherent and inalienable human dignity at every point in their journey with you. This is what we mean by *marketplace dignity*.

Using this definition, go back and look again at the anecdote about Neela that we shared earlier. Was she treated with the same value and respect as the customer who bought something different and engaged differently with the store?

So why should you make the effort? In Neela's anecdote, the man ahead of her walked away a happy customer. He had a good experience in the store and very likely received the post-purchase service he wanted. The store possibly made a decent profit from wiring his home. Neela's phone needs were smaller in scope, with negligible profit margins for the company. But who's to say whether the man came back to make further purchases after completing this big, one-off purchase? What we do know is that in the brief interaction that Neela experienced, she decided to cut ties with the brand for many years and told many others this story.

Treating your customers with dignity matters to you and your brand. In our research, talking to customers around the world and documenting their feedback, we have found that marketplace dignity matters for these reasons:

- **Marketplace dignity unlocks new value for your brand.** In our research, we have found evidence that when their dignity is affirmed, customers are happier with the services they receive, more likely to return to the business again, and more likely to recommend it to others.[2]
- **Marketplace dignity is important to consumers—and they remember when it is denied.** In our global surveys, respondents invariably agree that dignity matters in transactions. When consumers have a marketplace experience that compromises or denies their dignity in any way, the majority also say that they are less likely to return to that firm or business for future transactions.[3]
- **Marketplace dignity drives reputation and brand consistency.** If your stated values as an organization do not align with the customer experience, your brand reputation is at stake. Brands that talk openly about their values are at greater reputational risk when there are failures or shortcomings in marketplace dignity, however few or insignificant those experiences may appear to be.
- **Marketplace dignity can give you and your brand a seat at the table.** Firms that get marketplace dignity right not only reap benefits in terms of happy and loyal consumers, but are often in a position to elevate their brand by having a voice in the wider, societal debate.
- **Marketplace dignity brings benefits to your brand with minimal cost, effort, or outlay.** Treating your customers with dignity may sound abstract, but in reality, you can integrate and ensure marketplace dignity across every touch point of the customer journey both easily and efficiently. In this book, we will guide you through a three-lever framework that will help you do exactly that.[4]

Why We Wrote This Book

Cait Lamberton is Alberto I. Duran President's Distinguished Professor of Marketing at the Wharton School, University of Pennsylvania. Cait is a long-term observer of the ways in which behavioral science is applied in the real world. A disconnect between ideas and their implementation has consistently piqued her curiosity: Do the principles and insights provided by research really help organizations and communities in the long run? And do we have it right?

Cait brings her scholarship in the world of marketing and the customer journey to our discourse. Hers is the research, the academic perspective, and the discipline that bring the framework we've shared in this book: our Marketplace Dignity Framework, which we believe to be a major step forward in defining and operationalizing dignity as a driver of prosperity.

While working with students on an applied behavioral economics project, Cait met Neela Saldanha, now executive director of the Yale Research Initiative on Innovation and Scale (Y-RISE) at Yale University. Neela, who was the young mother you met earlier, had several years of experience in the private sector and shared Cait's concern about how behavioral science ideas were being picked up by organizations: some seemed to get it right more often than others, they found, but it wasn't always easy to figure out whether what they were doing right was clearly definable or scalable to other organizations. Neela began to take the lead in a lot of conversations related to behavioral science and ethics, and eventually, she and Cait started talking about the role of dignity in these situations.

Neela brings deep insight into the way both for-profit and non-profit organizations work from within—as a practitioner and a board member—and how they can change. For Neela, writing this book stems from a desire to wrap practicality around the concept of dignity and to make it work for real-world businesses.

Neela has always been a "hub for people who care about doing good things with behavioral science," in Cait's words. Neela introduced Cait to Tom Wein. Tom has been researching dignity since 2017, focused on the developing world and nonprofits. Tom is presently a director at IDinsight, a global advisory, data analytics, and research organization that helps global development leaders maximize their social impact. There, he leads the Dignity Initiative, bringing field research and partnerships to understand and implement the dignity agenda from the United States to Morocco to China—with the latest findings published in an annual Dignity Report.

As Neela puts it: Cait brings the theory, Tom the application, and she herself is somewhere in the middle, motivated by a translator's desire to demystify, to explain, and to share. When the three of us connected, more ideas emerged. The result is this book.

The three of us share this book with all those who hope to advance and understand dignity in their organizations. We think it will be of particular interest to those whose roles set the tone of relationships with customers, from product designers to marketers to retail managers. Leaders of these organizations, and those reflecting deeply on how to set a culture of respect, will also benefit, from chief executive officers (CEOs) and chief operating officers (COOs) to chief human resources officers (CHROs). We draw on examples from across sectors and from both the private sector to other institutions that serve people, like healthcare organizations and charities—readers working in all these areas will find material to reflect on. Finally, we have tried to take a global perspective, with case studies and data from the United States, the United Kingdom, India, Kenya, and many other places. We hope that readers all across the world will find familiar challenges and productive ways forward.

In This Book

Throughout this book, we'll share the stories of thinkers, companies, and organizations that are working to make dignity real in the marketplace, as well as some cautionary tales. These stories have inspired us, and we hope that they spark ideas about practical ways you can change your organization too.

Chapter 1 fleshes out the business case for marketplace dignity. For us, putting these ideas into practice is about creating a framework that enables you to treat every single customer in your base with the same consistent respect and consideration, no matter who they are or how they engage with your brand. In this chapter, we will dig deep into our Marketplace Dignity Framework and demonstrate how it works, using real-world examples that will help you situate theory in the context of practice.

In the chapters that follow, we will explore how to implement marketplace dignity, using our framework at each key point in your customer journey:

- **Pre-consumption:** How to segment, target, and advertise to your consumer groups with marketplace dignity as they begin to consider making a purchase
- **Evaluation:** How to engage customers who are evaluating their options with marketplace dignity
- **Consumption:** How to integrate marketplace dignity across the experience
- **Post-consumption:** How to ensure that your customers return time and time again.

Throughout these chapters, we will highlight cases where firms have done marketplace dignity well, with insights and tips on how to avoid the pitfalls.

In the closing chapters (chapter 6 and the epilogue), we'll invite you to join us in pursuing marketplace dignity, with practical recommendations on how to optimize your existing culture today and over the long term.

We hope that after reading this book, you will reach out to us to share your stories. Consistent with the idea of dignity itself, we hope to build a community of organizations committed to designing for dignity where we see, hear, recognize, and value one another's efforts and achievements.

We can be reached at marketplacedignity@gmail.com. We can't wait to hear from you.

Chapter 1

Marketplace Dignity
A Framework for the Whole of Your Customer Journey

In March 2013, PepsiCo ran a three-part advertising campaign promoting Mountain Dew. The campaign featured an anthropomorphic, talking goat called Felicia.

We first meet Felicia in a restaurant, where she is filmed beating up a human waitress who has run out of the soda. Over the next two spots, Felicia is seen escaping police arrest and then in a suspect lineup—alongside five Black men—where she is identified as the assailant by her bruised and terrified female victim.

Felicia the Goat garnered a lot of attention for PepsiCo. The advertising community hailed the concept as novel, unique, and "sticky," so to speak; some called it a "slice of crazed commercial perfection," and even the "best ad ever."[1]

But even as PepsiCo was basking in praise from industry press, a significant backlash was gathering momentum on social media. By the time the scholar and political analyst Boyce Watkins published an article denouncing the Felicia the Goat ad as "arguably the most racist commercial in history," the whole campaign had to be pulled.[2]

Here was a campaign, wrote Watkins, that not only portrayed Black men as suspects but put them "on par with animals." Mountain Dew had also managed to paint women as helpless victims, with no agency of their own, and the police as variously hapless incompetents or abusive thugs. The ads somehow managed to make goats look bad too. By May 1, PepsiCo had pulled Felicia from all its channels and issued a statement: "We apologize for the offensive video and take full responsibility—made a big mistake—we've removed it from all our channels. #fail."[3]

While it's hard to accurately quantify the hit to PepsiCo's brand equity as a result of the Mountain Dew imbroglio, it's clear that the company lost face very publicly in the aftermath. It is likely that it lost tens, if not hundreds, of thousands of dollars in marketing budget and untold hours spent by senior executives and decision-makers dealing with the reputational fallout. By then, an apology was the best option, no matter the cost.

The Business Case for Marketplace Dignity

Felicia the Goat and Mountain Dew illustrate what can happen when brands go out on a limb to differentiate a product or service but fail to factor in the dignity of their customer base in the marketplace. And PepsiCo is by no means alone in making this kind of mistake.

In 2018, two customers walked into a Starbucks coffee shop in Philadelphia to wait for a business acquaintance to join them for a coffee. An employee on duty accused them of loitering and trespassing. The same employee then called the police. Videos of these customers, both Black men, being led out of the store in handcuffs went viral, obliging CEO Kevin Johnson to issue a fulsome apology a few days later. This denial of dignity prompted national and international debate, winning Starbucks a spotlight in the dubious annals of reputational megacrises.[4]

Examples abound. The Dove brand from Unilever got into very public hot water in 2017 when it suggested that its body wash could turn a Black woman white. And the Beiersdorf brand Nivea clearly failed to get the memo in April that same year, when it told the world that "White is purity."[5]

In addition to racial bias and stereotypes, the researchers Jane Cunningham and Philippa Roberts analyze fifteen years of data in their book *Brandsplaining,* and they find "sneaky sexism" still rife in the global advertising industry: "Women of all ages have been told they need to be good, they need to be pleasing, they need to be pretty, they need to be passive. Those ideals have been held up as what women should be working towards. The role of brands is to help them achieve that and implicit within all of that is the criticism that says what you are is not enough."[6] Dove, for one, has worked hard to avoid this type of sexism, though no brand in the beauty industry can claim a perfect record in this area.[7]

If you get marketplace dignity wrong—when you deny the dignity of any customer at any inflection point in the customer journey, whether it's pre-consumption, evaluation, consumption, or post-consumption—you risk losing a lot, as PepsiCo, Starbucks, Unilever, and Beiersdorf did. Many of the examples we've shared here touch on race and gender, but there are myriad areas where dignity matters, as we shall see throughout this book.

Remember that firms that fail to respect and affirm the dignity of all their customers suffer the following consequences:

- **They lose customers.** Dignity matters to people, and its loss can spur strong emotional and psychological kickback. Consumers are highly likely to simply walk away from a business if their dignity is compromised in some way.
- **They lose new value.** The same customers who have walked away from your brand are also highly unlikely to come back anytime soon. They're even less likely to recommend you, your products, or your services to their peers—and perhaps more likely to write a negative review or speak up in criticism.
- **They lose face.** If your brand values don't match your customers' experiences, your reputation is at serious risk. All your talk about your values will be exposed as hypocrisy in practice.
- **They lose a seat at the table.** Firms that fail to treat customers with dignity also fail to build a community of loyalty and brand advocacy that can translate into greater clout and visibility beyond the marketplace. You lose the

chance to have a voice on broader societal issues that matter to your customers.[8]

And, as we said, there are multiple opportunities across your customer journey where you can either affirm or deny your customers' marketplace dignity. From pre-consumption to evaluation to consumption and on to post-consumption, you can get it very right—or very wrong.

Marketplace Dignity and the Customer Journey

Here's some additional food for thought.

In 2023, the professional services firm Accenture published a report detailing the most significant global consumer trends in the wake of the COVID-19 pandemic.

The biggest shift documented is people's increasing internalization of instability as the *norm*. In other words, your customers have become accustomed to living in a kind of *perma-crisis* that affects how they view, engage with, consume, and continue to interact with your brand.

According to Accenture, today's consumers are more likely than before to do one or more of these four things:

- **Fight:** Speak and act against what they see as injustice or unfairness.
- **Flight:** Shop around for alternatives.
- **Focus:** Stick to the things they feel they can control.
- **Freeze:** Switch off and disengage entirely.[9]

In the current uncertain, perma-crisis environment, if you want to capture the pre-consumption attention of your customers, warrant their evaluation of your offering, engage with them as consumers, and build their post-purchase loyalty—we would recommend that you think about the following questions:

- How can you demonstrate unequivocally that you are consistently just and fair in your values and practices?
- How can you offer products, services, and experiences that map to what customers value, want, and need?
- How can you ensure that they are empowered, feel in control, and have agency in their interactions with you?

Getting these things right at every point of the customer journey, such that your customers don't fight, turn to flight, lose focus, or freeze, might need you to stop and rethink what you (think you) know or understand about your customers.

So how do you do this? And in your efforts to differentiate your brand, products, and services, how do you avoid the all-too-easy mistakes and pitfalls that can see even the biggest companies labeled racist, misogynistic, disrespectful, or horribly out of touch with their customer base?

The good news is that through research led by Cait and others, and our combined years of investigating marketplace dignity, we have come to identify three distinct levers you can use for your own real-world marketing and customer care practices that will help you affirm marketplace dignity to every customer in their journey with you and your brand. And based on this research, we have built a framework that integrates these three levers consistently and coherently at every juncture of that journey. We call this the **Marketplace Dignity Framework**.[10]

In the chapters to come, we will show you how to use the Marketplace Dignity Framework at each of the following phases of the customer journey:

- **Pre-consumption:** Segment, target, and advertise to your consumer groups with their dignity in mind.
- **Evaluation:** Engage consumers while respecting their dignity.
- **Consumption:** Create experiences that honor your customers' dignity.

- **Post-consumption:** Ensure your customers return time and time again.

Take a look at Figure 1.1 to see how this maps out.

But before we get into details, let us just share a few last thoughts on dignity so we're very clear on what marketplace dignity is, and *what it isn't*.

Remember how, in the introduction to this book, we asked you to consider how dignity shouldn't be confused with things like self-esteem or pride? We think it's also important to underscore that, from a corporate perspective, designing for dignity is not the same as having "purpose" or trading off customer centricity.

Doing generally good things—be it having a vision, articulating a higher purpose, driving for sustainability, or obsessing about broadening your social impact—does not automatically equate to respecting your customers' dignity. You can do the right thing in the wrong way. But a focus on dignity can help you ensure that you truly deliver on your purpose in ways that bring value not only to your target consumers, but to the marketplace as a whole. As Daniel Lubetzky, the

Figure 1.1. Marketplace Dignity and the Customer Journey

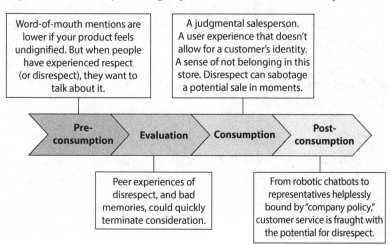

founder of KIND snacks, says, "I have never seen a brand's mission advance successfully without an underlying framework of values driving it."[11]

Similarly, advancing dignity need not conflict with thoughtful and effective business techniques. Providing different offerings to customers with different levels of engagement is okay, and sometimes that kind of customer centricity is exactly what is most respectful.[12] The goal here is to ensure that you work to have a minimum level of respect for each customer. That's a topic we get into in more detail later in the book.

Remember this: Dignity can be defined as being inherently valued and respected by others for who we are as human beings. By this definition, firms that affirm the marketplace dignity of their customers are those that show their customers that they value and respect them—regardless of where they sit in terms of priority, what they buy from you, or how they choose to engage with your brand.

We contend that *purpose* and *values* alone are not enough if you truly want to assert and affirm your customers' dignity. You need a framework—one that is built on the constituent pillars or levers of marketplace dignity—to ensure that dignity is systematically affirmed and not denied throughout your customers' engagement and interaction with your brand.

This is where our Marketplace Dignity Framework comes into play. Let's look at what this framework entails and how it works.

The Marketplace Dignity Framework

Over the past seven years, we have conducted twenty-five large-scale studies across the United States, Africa, Latin America, and India, interviewing tens of thousands of people about their personal experiences with marketplace dignity.

In collectively listening to what scholars, business practitioners, and consumers have told us, we have identified three concrete and actionable pillars or levers you can use to evaluate and effectively design for dignity.[13]

Figure 1.2. The Marketplace Dignity Framework

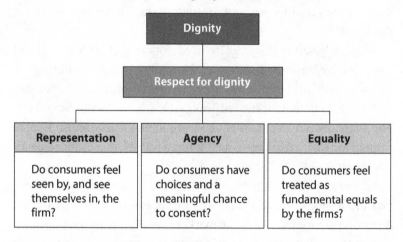

These levers, depicted in figure 1.2, are

- Representation: Feeling seen and heard
- Agency: Feeling in control
- Equality: Feeling treated as an equal

Let's break these three levers down further to understand how each of them functions in the context of marketplace dignity and your customers' experiences.

Representation

When people feel seen and heard by the companies they interact with, we call it *representation*. Representation also happens when people see and hear others who are like them within that company. And when this happens in a way that is both *authentic and accurate,* they know their individual and group identities are *recognized and valued.*

Representation can be simple to do and measure. It can be something as straightforward as using a customer's name. Science tells us that hearing our own name has a powerful and instant neural impact: it relays the sense that someone is more interested in us, that we matter to them, and that they're paying attention to us. It also aligns to our capacity for "self-representation," which is something that comes naturally to us human beings.[14]

While representation seems like it can be relatively simple to do, it can be extremely risky when things go wrong. Science tells us that consumers who are identified correctly feel more respected. But it also tells us that the opposite happens when consumers are mis-identified.[15] Mispronounce your customer's name, and all your good intentions can be instantly corrupted—especially if you continue to use the wrong name without correcting yourself (and particularly after you have been corrected by the customer). Misusing names can make people feel that their identity is misunderstood. Worse still, it can leave them feeling alienated.[16]

Mispronouncing a customer's name is one thing. Misrepresenting the identity of an entire group of customers is even worse. Take the case of the UK food store Tesco. In 2015, Tesco attempted to reach Muslim shoppers celebrating the end of Ramadan. Their Liverpool Street store in London dedicated an entire aisle display to a brand of "smokey bacon" flavored potato chips, bearing the celebratory message: Ramadan Mubarak. Those who designed this promotion failed to recognize that pork products are prohibited foods for Muslims.

The store in question services shoppers in the area of the East London Mosque, one of the biggest centers of worship for European Muslims. The display quickly went viral via Twitter, forcing Tesco to scrap the campaign and issue an apology: "We are proud to offer a wide range of meals and products to meet the needs of our customers during Ramadan. We recognize these Pringles weren't in the most suitable place, and our store colleagues have now moved them."

The episode surely left a bad taste in the mouths of customers and cost Tesco time, effort, and good relations with the local community.[17]

Representation can be hazardous for firms that (even with the best will in the world) end up pandering to stereotypes, banding people together, or imbuing entire groups with a single, simplified identity.

Remember Felicia the Goat? We know that Black men are under-represented within certain identity groups: for instance, as users of technology, playable characters in video games, and consumers of luxury goods. But they are overrepresented or stereotyped as anonymous gangsters, drug users or, at the other extreme, as pro athletes or superheroes. Meanwhile, women are typically represented as helpless victims, prone to the whims and decisions of men.[18] The Mountain Dew ads played to all of these stereotypes and others, misrepresenting an entire race and gender in PepsiCo's efforts to be edgy or amusing.

Tesco and PepsiCo are by no means alone in making the occasional blunder on customer representation. A 2019 study of popular global films reveals that while Muslims make up around 25% of the world's population, they accounted for fewer than 2% of speaking movie characters—the overwhelming majority of whom are depicted as subservient, outsiders, or "bad guys."[19]

Studies of advertising surface similarly dismal findings about people with disabilities and the lesbian, gay, bisexual, transgender, and queer/questioning (LGBTQ) community, who collectively make up fewer than 1% of the characters portrayed in campaigns outside of Pride Month. When LGBTQ representation spikes (primarily coinciding with Pride celebrations), it is often seen as inauthentic.[20]

In trying to represent their customers faithfully, firms can all too often end up misrepresenting, underrepresenting, or failing to represent their customers altogether. And in an age of mass information, it only gets more complex. As firms go digital, the imperative to respect users' preferences in terms of being seen or heard—to affirm their representational dignity—only becomes more acute; and easier to ignore. In 2018, then–Facebook CEO Mark Zuckerberg famously boasted that his company not only tracked its own users' data, it even tracked the behavior of consumers without an active Facebook account[21]—forcing people to be seen without their consent, and thereby failing on two pillars of the Marketplace Dignity Framework: representation and agency (which we discuss next).

So how do you get representation right? For a start, representation has relevance beyond just the pre-consumption and evaluation phases of your customer journey. From advertising to product design to customer service, representation needs to be a pillar of marketplace dignity.

Who is getting representation right? And what can you learn from them?

Getting It Right on Representation:
The Tricycle Cafe & Bicycle Shop

In Conshohocken, a town of 9,000 in Pennsylvania, Adena Brewington-Brown, Michael Brown, and Isaiah Urbino opened a new bicycle store in 2021. The store was born of their love of cycling, which the three had been doing since they were kids. It was also the product of their frustration with a world that seemed built to exclude them as people of color; Adena and Michael are Black, and Isaiah is Latino.

Adena and Michael were interviewed by a local newspaper, *GridPhilly*. Michael shared, "You know, in a lot of shops, you'd see the advertisements on the wall. You look on the wall and all you saw were middle-aged white guys that were built like a string bean," he said. "That's the demographic that has been in cycling for quite some time."[22]

"We're minorities within the cycling community, and we want to have a safe space for all people," shared Adena.[23]

For the Tricycle Cafe & Bicycle Shop, customer representation is intersectional. The founders want to make sure that people of different races, genders, sexual orientations, and body types all find a welcoming community in cycling. But is it paying off in business terms?

When Hurricane Ida hit the town in September 2021, the business had been open just two months. Even so, locals rallied to donate more than $30,000 to cover insurance deductibles, lost revenues, and cleanup. Since opening in July 2021, nearly every online review has been a five-star rave. In our experience and work with industry, we can honestly say there aren't many businesses who could count on that much loyalty that fast.

So representation is the first lever in our Marketplace Dignity Framework, and in the next several chapters, we'll look at things you can do to ensure equitable and faithful representation at the various points of your customer journey. Representation, however, is not enough.

Let's look at the second lever in our Marketplace Dignity Framework: **Agency**.

Agency

Some of you may remember Burger King's flagship campaign from the 1970s. "Have it your way" came out in 1974 as a way of differentiating Burger King from its rival, McDonald's, by tapping into customers' sense of individuality and desire for control. "We may be King," ran the ad, "but you, my friend, are the almighty ruler."

Agency is what happens when customers feel in control. When we feel that we have options and a meaningful chance to consent about our experiences with a brand, we feel empowered, enfranchised, and in control.

In practice, agency is often a form of customization per Burger King's exhortation to customers to build burgers to their own preferences. But firms should be careful about taking the customization = agency equation too far. When people have *too many* choices, it can become dizzying and overwhelming for them. The "paradox of choice" is well known and shows up in the marketplace: a UK survey showed that 83% of shoppers who abandoned a purchase did so because they were overwhelmed with too many options.[24]

Such overwhelming choice costs organizations money. The US healthcare system, for example, is so complex that 52% of people are unable to navigate it. Health insurers and employers spend almost $5 billion every year on administration fees alone to deal with consumers who have low health literacy, cannot comprehend the national user site, and therefore require assistance getting what they need when they need it.[25]

Helping consumers navigate choice becomes even more important in uncertain times and can be a source of advantage. And some savvy retail players are enthusiastically leveraging this to their competitive advantage.

Take the US grocery chain Trader Joe's. This is an organization that has been consistently lauded for empowering its customers. Trader Joe's doesn't overload people with choices. According to a well-known study on choice by the Columbia Business School professor and researcher Sheena Iyengar, customers are much more likely to feel empowered to make a choice when the options in front of them don't overwhelm them in any way.[26] It's no coincidence that Trader Joe's carries around a tenth of the product stock-keeping units (SKUs) of a typical grocery store or supermarket.[27] However, these fewer options are of a consistently high quality and carry prices that can neither be fudged nor misunderstood. Trader Joe's never runs sales, nor do they offer their customers coupons: what you see is what you get in their stores.[28] This is a store that stocks a fraction of the products that their rival Whole Foods does yet sells twice as much per square foot.[29]

Choice matters, as does choice overload. But what about another "c"—consent?

In the twenty-first century, user consent has become a burning issue for organizations, regulators, and customers alike. Yet many companies seem to drag their feet when asking for it.

Users are invited to consent to their data being collected, but in ways that essentially and all too often deny us our dignity. Terms and conditions are presented to us in ways that we cannot easily comprehend. One leading organization offers its users a terms and conditions document to read and sign that runs more than 18,000 words—about half the length of this book. It would take two hours and twenty-seven minutes to read it from start to finish.[30]

It seems that less-than-scrupulous companies will do anything to get their hands on customer data. Worse still are the issues of hidden fees, lock-in subscriptions, and so-called dark-pattern cross-selling. The US retail bank Wells Fargo found itself embroiled in scandal when it was discovered that 1.5 million personal accounts and over 565,000 credit cards had been opened and activated without customer consent—a crisis that saw the bank obliged to pay $185 million in fines.[31]

Of course, many firms are purposefully and actively getting it right: showing ways forward that respect consent and dignity, and posting encouraging numbers in the process.

The Germany-based meal-kit company HelloFresh maintains that the best way to serve the bottom line is to put customers in charge of their own consent and subscriptions, and to give them the easy option of pausing their subscriptions, or even canceling them, whenever they want.[32] The result? The company has experienced skyrocketing growth, posting 7.6 billion euros in revenue for FY2022, with "more than 1 billion meals shipped."[33]

Empowering your customers, respecting their ability to choose, soliciting their consent, and giving them agency: All this is critical to asserting and affirming their marketplace dignity. And we'll show you how to do this across the customer journey in the chapters to come.

Now let's look at the third and final lever in our Marketplace Dignity Framework: **Equality**.

Equality

Equality happens when people feel that companies and other individuals see them as peers. Equality also happens when the power differentials across various customer groups, and between customers and the firm itself, are minimized, when everyone receives the same even-handed and nondiscriminatory consideration and treatment.

Although sensitivity to inequality is one of our earliest developmental milestones as human beings, we often fail to proactively build, safeguard, and communicate equality to our customers as organizations. Countless women and people of color that we have surveyed and spoken with over the years share stories of belittlement in all kinds of consumer encounters. Remember Neela's interaction with the phone-store clerk and how she felt when she was given less attention and respect than the customer who preceded her in line? It's a story we've heard hundreds if not thousands of times: everyday inequity and discrimination in all kinds of contexts.

When the legendary Apple designer Don Norman took corporate America to task for failing to represent the older consumer, he was really onto something. Leaflets with instructions in tiny, impossible-to-read print; hard-to-open bottle tops; and stylish phones that were a nightmare for hand-eye coordination were denying the dignity of an entire generation, as he wrote in a now-famous op-ed for *Fast Company*: "Designers and companies of the world, you are badly serving an ever-growing segment of your customer base, a segment that you too will one day inhabit. Isn't it time to reform: to make things that are functional and stylish, useable and accessible? Every ailment that I described that impacts the elderly is also present in people of all ages. Designs that make it easier for elderly people often are of equal value for younger people. In fact, for everyone. Help the elderly, and the results will help many more, including yourself, someday."[34]

Actual human interactions in stores, restaurants, hotels, or offices are one thing. But inequality can be built into products and services in ways that we may not even realize. When Norman complained, it's unlikely that he was taking issue with companies that purposefully sought to belittle or disrespect older customers. But whether these organizations were aware of it or not, the message they were sending this demographic was this: We're focused on serving younger people; your needs are less important to us than theirs. Norman shouted about marketplace dignity from the rooftops, and others have taken heed and followed suit.[35]

World Central Kitchen is a US-based nongovernmental organization (NGO) founded by chef José Andrés in 2010 that provides food to people displaced by natural and human-made crises—the overwhelming majority of them in emerging countries. As they declare on their website, "We know that a nourishing meal in a time of crisis is so much more than a plate of food—it's hope, it's dignity, and it's a sign that someone cares." World Central Kitchen ensures delicious, chef-prepared meals in close coordination with affected communities.[36]

For this company, customers are equals. Affirming their marketplace dignity is written into the DNA of the organization. Of course, the nonprofit sector in some cases might be more geared to the affirmation of dignity than others—though there are many examples of charities patronizing and demeaning those they serve. All sectors of society can do more to get it right when it comes to dignity.

As we have emphasized before, equality does not require that everyone be treated in precisely the same way. There are plenty of good reasons for offering benefits to loyal customers, tailoring bids for different customer segments, or offering premium and budget versions of your product. In fact, those are good ways of employing strategies of representation and agency. But *explaining differential treatment in ways that are seen as fair* can help consumers accept segment-based treatment.

A good example of this is the bronze, silver, and platinum model used by airlines. Customers are bracketed according to the number of air miles they fly, and as they notch up more miles, they progress toward different categories of benefits, perks, and treatment. Similarly, customers tend not to get annoyed by differential offers to the elderly or to early-bird subscribers. Different treatment, different prices— but still fair. Other companies like Happy Money credit lenders offer a form of personalization in prepayment rates that is contingent on customers' individual needs and profiles, while still being fair to all— an approach that has led to interest from investors in funding their growth.[37]

Remember that the equality lever simply requires that you do not proactively diminish the essential importance of each customer, and that you do what you can to minimize the power differential between you. In the chapters to come, we'll explore different ways that targeted and tailored services can be provided using strategies and tactics that preserve equality, and thus protect your customers' dignity at every stage of their journey with you.

The Marketplace Dignity Framework: A Final Word Before We Begin

In our research, we have seen that the three levers of our Marketplace Dignity Framework recur in traditions of dignity around the world.

Almost every society, philosophy, and religion has had some idea of dignity. And from Nairobi to Bangalore (Bengaluru), Chicago to Bogotá, these three levers to affirm dignity are the same.

In March 2020, we ran a study. We surveyed 400 Americans this time, and sure enough, when people feel they have been recognized, given agency, and treated as an equal, that's when they tell us their dignity has been respected.[38] We ran the study again. And again. And every time, these three factors matter.[39] Later, we ran it in Nigeria and India too and found the same results.[40]

The three levers of our Marketplace Dignity Framework are backed by research and undergirded by the evidence we have found in the field. They are also pragmatic. The three levers will provide practical and actionable suggestions on the paths your firm might follow to assure marketplace dignity for your customers at every touch point in their journey with you and your brand.

But our three levers are not to be followed blindly. Sometimes they get in each other's way: Customers want to be known and represented, but they don't want their privacy invaded. They like options, but they don't like the idea that someone else got special treatment. They want to be treated as an equal, but they also might like the option to pay for the privilege of skipping the line. They want things explained to them, but they also want to finish a transaction and get on with their day. Luckily, there's an acid test for all this: Your customer decides.

If your customers think they have been treated disrespectfully, then they *have been* treated disrespectfully. That's not them being fickle; it's them expressing their full and complex humanity, in ways to which businesses have to adapt.

At the end of the day, if you want to know what's truly respectful— what you do or don't do that affirms dignity—ask your customers.

When you're getting it wrong, if you take a moment to listen, people will soon tell you. And they'll appreciate that you asked.

Now, let's look at your customer journey.

In chapter 2, we'll explore how to use our Marketplace Dignity Framework in the pre-consumption phase: techniques and tactics you can use to affirm representation, agency, and equality in advertising and marketing.

Chapter 1: Key Insights and Takeaways

- Dignity matters to your customers.
- It's easy to get it wrong: Some of the biggest and best-established brands have denied the dignity of their customers at times.
- It's also easier than you might think to get it right.
- Our Marketplace Dignity Framework offers three levers you can use to affirm your customers' dignity: representation, agency, and equality.
- You can use the Marketplace Dignity Framework at every point in your customer journey.

Chapter 2

Marketplace Dignity at the Pre-Consumption Phase
Starting with Respect

R emember the Apple designer, Don Norman, from chapter 1? Remember how he stood up for the marketplace dignity of older customers: how he took issue with leaflets with too-small-to-read print and impossible-to-open bottle tops? Norman was even vocal in his criticism of Apple's designs, penning a no-holds-barred piece for *Fast Company* that flagged certain "crimes" against usability.[1]

Nonetheless, Apple has had its good moments. Some of you may remember their iconic 1984 ad for the Macintosh computer. Titled "Nineteen Eighty-Four" and directed by the acclaimed director Ridley Scott, the spot references George Orwell's novel of the same name. It opens with a line of whey-faced automatons marching in unison to the voice of a leader who is depicted spewing propaganda on a large screen. Suddenly a heroine appears in glorious technicolor—a powerful athlete, brandishing a hammer. With a single shot-put throw, she smashes the video screen, shattering the uniformity and offering the masses a (Macintosh-shaped) path out of Orwellian despair.

Apple's "Nineteen Eighty-Four" ad was hailed as a masterpiece. Within three months of its first airing during the 1984 Super Bowl TV broadcast, the company sold more than 70,000 of its new computers. The ad garnered a clutch of awards, including the best Super Bowl spot in forty years. To this day, it is considered one of the greatest feats of advertising and an absolute touchstone for the industry.[2]

"Nineteen Eighty-Four" was skillfully shot, edited, and produced. The concept is clever, and it's pleasingly pithy in its delivery. But any ad can be clever. Felicia the Goat enjoyed her moment in the sunshine of virality and notoriety, but that campaign was short-lived. We believe the enduring appeal of this spot is also partly due to its clear appeal to human dignity.

Rather than hyper-focusing on their product's technological benefits, Apple sparked curiosity and triggered engagement by tapping into a universal, shared need to be seen, heard, and empowered. Rather than leaning into stereotypes that group people together, or at the other extreme, undermining privacy in the interest of micro-targeting, Apple appealed to our shared desire for representation, agency, and equality.

As Apple did in this case, we believe that you need to prioritize and affirm your customers' marketplace dignity in your advertising and marketing efforts such that you appeal to their sense of representation, agency, and equality. This is the phase when you are trying to reach consumers before they have experienced your product, and when the tone of the relationship is set.

In this chapter, we will break down how you do this using our Marketplace Dignity Framework. We will also share a set of diagnostic questions that you can use to assess your existing pre-consumption strategies and tools and to find new and creative ways to affirm representation, agency, and equality.

Representation at the Pre-Consumption Phase

Remember that representation is about our human need to be seen and heard as individuals on our own terms. When we fail to see customers (especially customers from groups that have been historically excluded) in ways that affirm their worth, when we deny them voice, or when we violate their freedom *not* to be seen, we run a high risk of undermining their dignity and losing out.[3]

When Hindustan Unilever Limited launched Axe deodorant in India in 1999, the campaign depicted men, their target audience, as nerdy losers. Women were simultaneously delineated as one-dimensional sex objects whom the product was supposed to attract—and who existed solely for the pleasure of these nerdy, loser men. It was a segmentation strategy that played to none of the strengths of the product's potential customers and underpinned a series of ads that were so offensive they were eventually banned by Indian authorities. One such ad, "Chocolate Man," which was taken off air soon after release, saw a man shapeshift into a walking, talking chocolate bar after spraying himself with Axe.[4] So irresistible was this anthropomorphic candy bar that women couldn't stop biting chunks from him on buses and streets. In one fell swoop, the company had managed to objectify men and reduce women to simple atavists—not really how anyone of any gender wants to be seen.

What could have been done differently?

Before you settle on a segmentation strategy that provides insight for your advertising campaign, we recommend that you stop and sense-check your ideas through the dignity lens for all customers, not only your target audience. In the case of "Chocolate Man," asking both men and women their reactions to the ad and focusing specifically on the dignity levers might have brought forth valuable information that allowed the company to understand the target market in a way that truly captured their needs and wants. Further, the company would probably have gained a richer understanding about how a product that is both personal and self-expressive could better affirm consumers' dignity. And indeed, Unilever pledged in 2016 to do away with sexist ads after finding that 40% of women did not identify at all with the women they saw in advertising.[5] In 2019, a new set of ads for Axe focused on redefining masculinity. As Sharan Saikumar, the creative director of Arré (the content agency), said, "Brands are taking progressive and responsible stands today not just because they should, but because they want to be part of conversations that the youth is having today."[6] In this case, Unilever followed societal trends, but with a dignity lens, they could have led these conversations a few years earlier.

Representation matters. And it needs to be authentic, it needs to be based on actual people, and it needs to be inclusive. At the pre-consumption phase, segmentation and targeting directly relate to the question of who a firm sees and who they therefore decide is worth addressing (and to whom they should listen). In our experience working with firms, segmentation schemes sometimes split a market by some criteria and not others, no matter how sophisticated these schemes might be. As a result, there is always the potential that a firm will focus on criteria that fail to recognize the true value, story, or priorities of all their consumers.

Axe is just one story in the annals of misrepresentation in pre-consumption segmentation. But there are so many more instances of brands getting it wrong that they are hard to enumerate. We know that women are overtargeted in the household products industry, while they are undertargeted as purchasers of cars and automobiles.[7] Studies show that minorities and low-income Americans are under-targeted in consumption around environmental products or services, and yet these demographic groups evince a high degree of concern about the environment in public opinion surveys. Black communities suffer more than their fair share of this kind of flawed representation.[8]

In their attempt to ensure that Black Americans felt represented, seen, heard, and valued, PepsiCo inadvertently found itself again on their back foot in 2017. The Pepsi "Live for Now '' campaign featured the model and influencer Kendall Jenner, a white cisgender woman. In the ad, a white police officer is seen monitoring a protest that is starting to get out of hand. As tensions escalate, Jenner hands the officer a can of Pepsi. The officer takes the drink and breaks into a broad smile, suggesting that a can of Pepsi can resolve any conflict. What this ad fails to acknowledge are the myriad complexities surrounding police and community relations in the United States—with the Black community in particular.

Firms all too often fail to see their customers in their totality, precisely when they are most intent on trying to make them feel seen.

The commercial was seen as trivializing the Black Lives Matter movement and the lives of the people involved. Further, in using a model who identifies and is identified as white as the heroine, the company was deemed by many to "erase" Black women who had been instrumental in civil rights protests—a spectacular failure in terms of representation. As Karen Attiah of the *Washington Post* put it: "[The ad] represents a pervasive and persistent white liberal fantasy of U.S. protest politics that trivializes the long and oftentimes dangerous work of resistance and protest, and at the same time marginalizes people of color who often are the drivers of such protests, at great costs to their lives and livelihoods. What irks me, as a Black woman, the most about Pepsi's attempt to make Protest the New Black is that it completely excludes black women from any meaningful part of the protest action."[9]

So how do you get representation right? In 2017, Heineken released "Worlds Apart," a campaign predicated on the notion that when you bring diverse ideas together, you can achieve positive outcomes. The brand filmed six strangers paired up to follow a set of instructions and build a bar together. As they work, they become aware of the fact that their partner holds diametrically different political views from their own. Once the bar is built, each partnership is given the option to simply walk away or to stay and discuss their differences over a bottle of Heineken beer. All choose to sit and talk their differences out.

The "Worlds Apart" commercial doesn't seek to suggest that the beer can produce instant solutions to a complex problem. Nor does it underrepresent or erase different target audiences: The ads show a mix of both liberal and conservative audiences without privileging either. Instead, this campaign situates the moment of consumption quite realistically: The beer is depicted as something that can facilitate conversations.

Heineken's detractors argue that the "Worlds Apart" campaign is overly simplistic. However, most agree that consumers and products are represented in a way that seeks to look below the surface and unearth more of the complexity and authenticity therein. *Fast Company* hailed the advertisement as the "antidote" to Pepsi's "Live for Now"[10]

All this is testimony to the work that Heineken put in by working behind the scenes with researchers from the UK's Goldsmiths, University of London, and The Human Library, a think tank that works to debunk stereotypes.[11] As a result of this work and the resulting campaign, Heineken saw its reach on social media skyrocket and sales of its beer increase by more than 7%. A majority of customers surveyed in the wake of the campaign reported that "Heineken was a brand for them."[12]

As you are segmenting audiences and thinking about advertising, marketing, and promotional campaigns for your own products or services, a very useful tool for your reference is the Dignified Storytelling Handbook, an initiative launched by Dubai Cares and the African Union, among other partners. Dignified Storytelling identifies ten principles or statements you can use to help ensure you achieve more authentic representation of other people.[13] Here are those principles—think about how you might apply them in your own pre-consumption processes around representation:

1. **It's not my story:** Amplifies contributors' voices and experiences, honoring their wishes on what story is told and how it is told.
2. **I do no harm.** Applies a "do no harm" ethic to all actions.
3. **We are all multidimensional.** Treats each individual as a whole person and every community as dynamic and multidimensional.
4. **Consent is more than paperwork.** Dignified storytelling obtains informed, full, and freely given consent from contributors.
5. **I am biased (repeat).** Acknowledges and mitigates biases, stereotypes, social stigmas, and power differences.
6. **I do my homework.** Values local social, moral, and cultural norms.

7. **I am empathetic.** Considers the impact of stories on individuals, communities, and the natural environment.

8. **I protect others' data like it's my own.** Processes and manages content responsibly, in line with existing data protection guidance and laws.

9. **Truth over headlines.** Depicts realities with accuracy and authenticity.

10. **A story can change the world.** Empowers and inspires both contributors and audiences to work toward positive change.[14]

A Short Word About Representation and Aspiration

When you are segmenting your audience at the pre-consumption phase, be careful to pitch for the aspirational, not the reductive.

Plenty of firms and organizations will offer discounts as a means of engaging customers, but promotions like senior discounts can backfire if they signal to one segment of your customer base that they are somehow economically worse off or less empowered than others. Be careful of unintended consequences if you match promotions to things like age. Offer all your consumers a simple discount valid for every segment, and you bypass the risk of denying the dignity of some of them. As *Time* columnist Brad Tuttle writes: "So even though Baby Boomers love getting a deal as much as the next person, they hate the idea of getting a 'senior discount'—which is tantamount to accepting the fact that they're officially old." Tuttle calls this an "odd phenomenon, in which Baby Boomers are torn between wanting a discount for their seniority in the population and refusing to admit to senior status." This struggle is why "AARP, formerly the American Association of Retired Persons, welcomes 'members' (not 'seniors') starting at age 50, and all the perks are 'member benefits,' not 'senior benefits.'"[15]

Everyone wants to be represented in a way that is positive or that matches an aspirational view that they have of themselves. The founder and CEO of BMe Community, Trabian Shorters, calls this "asset framing." It boils down to "defining people by their aspirations and contributions, before you get into their challenges," says Shorters. And it's an approach that he urges firms to adopt: "You've got to say: What is it we're investing in? We're not investing in [things like] poverty. Who invests in poverty? You're not trying to grow poverty. You're trying to invest in people's aspirations towards wealth; you're trying to invest in people's will to make a better future for their children or their community."[16]

University of Michigan psychologist and researcher Catherine Thomas agrees. She and her colleagues conducted a 2020 study looking at how communities in Kenya responded to the naming options for a charitable business skills program that was about to be launched there. Of the prospective names—"Poverty Alleviation," "Individual Empowerment," or "Community Empowerment—it was the latter (community empowerment) that made people feel more self-empowerment and less stigma. Respondents told Thomas that "Community Empowerment '' made people feel more motivated to build their business skills and drive for the kind of social mobility they aspired to achieve.[17]

Representing your customers *how they want to be represented* is the key here. And we believe that means taking measures to have your customers drive the design of your marketing research. Involving your customers can help ensure that your segmentation efforts are rooted in their self-understanding rather than labels or ideas that you impose on them.

In your advertising, marketing, and promotional efforts, we believe you should strive to recognize the importance, depth, and authenticity of actual, lived experience. Finding ways to allow your customers to identify themselves and share their individual experiences with you and your brand can make all the difference. You might even go beyond tried-and-tested measures like closed surveys and use more wide-ranging and open-ended methodologies, such as those deployed by the likes of Miele or HTC. Both companies have gone the extra mile, quite literally spending time living with customers and observing their habits, needs, challenges, and wants in detail—a practice known as *ethnography* in market research, and which has its roots in anthropology. The insights yielded by spending actual time with real-life customers can have a direct impact on the way you market your goods and services.[18]

This discussion grounds the first set of questions that we'd propose you use to evaluate your pre-consumption efforts through the lens of marketplace dignity. Ask yourself the following questions:

- Does your customer segmentation (in development, labeling, and description) and advertising or promotional work emphasize not only your customers' weaknesses and challenges, but also their strengths? How would consumers describe themselves? Could any of your current classifications make your customers feel disrespected in some way, and if so, how?
- Does your advertising or promotional activity acknowledge more than one story? Or do you tend to impose a single story on all members of a group? Are the members of your group meaningfully different, and would that group recognize those members' differences?
- In terms of how you communicate with different groups, are you working with those groups to create a set of principles? A resource that we believe could help you here is the ANA Educational Foundation, which publishes on race and ethnicity in advertising and marketing.[19]

Agency at the Pre-Consumption Phase

In 2020, COVID-19 severely curtailed people's freedom and control. Lockdowns, travel restrictions, mask wearing, and social distancing limited our ability to interact, work, and live under our own agency. Some decision-makers responded to this novel situation in ways that sought to affirm dignity. The secretary-general of the United Nations (UN), António Guterres, formulated a plan to secure access to medical care and other resources for older cohorts in particular—an attempt to recognize the inherent agency and dignity of the elderly.

"Let's not treat older people as invisible or powerless," Guterres wrote in his policy briefing.[20] However, other organizations were not quite as forthcoming in their efforts to respect people's agency.

Certainly, we saw ample cautionary tales in the actions taken by policymakers, who did little to affirm people's sense of agency, choice, or control—particularly in terms of vaccination against COVID-19. Indeed, the US Centers for Disease Control and Prevention acknowledged their failure to communicate in ways that made people feel empowered, noting that public health officials may lack enough marketing knowledge to deliver well-designed messaging.[21]

In a time when so many felt deprived of agency, firms might not be blamed for leaving a great deal of choice out of the pre-consumption portion of a consumer journey. And science also shows that firms can easily get this wrong. Recent research reveals that consumers have such a strong need to preserve a sense of agency that they will stop buying a product if marketers explicitly link it too strongly to a specific identity. One study invited participants to share how much environmental issues mattered to them. They then had to choose between two brands of soap: "Charlies: The Only Good Choice for Green Consumers" and "Charlies: A Good Choice for Green Consumers." To the researchers' surprise, "The Only Good Choice for Green Consumers" had significantly less success than the other brand, even where participants had expressed high levels of concern about the environment. Why? Because they had underestimated the effect of losing agency.[22]

Firms and organizations of all types risk denying the pre-consumption agency of their customers in different ways. One is by disguising the intent of advertisements or promotions. Such sleight of hand makes it impossible for customers to understand the priority that they should afford to a given message, thus denying them attentional agency.

For example, a Burger King ad run in 2017 included a verbal message designed to activate people's Google Home devices in answer to the question, "What is the Whopper burger?" Within three hours, the ad no longer activated any Google devices because Google (which had not been consulted about the ad) caught on and recognized the threat the ad created. As Bob Gilbreath, chief of the marketing tech company Ahalogy, noted: "Most people don't trust advertising, and having advertising continually listen to what happens in our homes is scary." Further, Burger King seemed to deny that the ad was invasive, showing a surprising amount of tone-deafness for a firm that sometimes gets agency right.[23]

A way to better incorporate agency into the pre-consumption phase of your customer journey is to reject such techniques and instead offer transparency and freedom of attention. While it may seem counterintuitive, a dignity-based advertising design is honest about its intentions and provides multiple opportunities to opt out or skip advertisements easily. To some extent, customers have always maintained this control; "zipping" and "zapping" between channels, as well as trips to the refrigerator during commercial breaks may have frustrated advertisers, but it has also given viewers a certain dignity of choice.

We would suggest that you should resist the temptation to use technology in ways that take away this kind of freedom. And while some may argue that doing this will decrease your return on advertising, recent data suggests quite the opposite: Consumers will avoid sources that do *not* allow skipping. More generally, consumers may be willing to engage with ads that are relevant, not intrusive, and incentivized to give them more control, such as rewarded video ads.[24]

Nudging customers to consume advertisements can be effective. Done well, they can give users plenty of autonomy and choice. However, a common practice in advertising is to use nontransparent nudges, in which consumers may not be aware of the intention of the ad—such as using a decoy that presents an option that is similar but inferior to the target option in order to get people to purchase the target. But this kind of practice reduces agency by directing consumers away from the item that would meet their needs. The behavioral scientists Leonhard K. Lades and Liam Delaney have this to say about such practices: "When nudges make people feel as if they were not treated like an independent human being capable of making sensible decisions, these nudges can come across as insults and as being disrespectful."[25]

In the short term, ads like this may be good for business—they have been shown to increase retailer profits. But over time, these kinds of tactics reduce agency and deny dignity; and remember what we told you that you and your firm stand to lose when you deny dignity. Over the longer term, you can risk losing customers, losing new value, losing face, and losing a seat at the table on the issues that matter to your client base.

We would strongly urge you to be brave enough to rely on the quality of your product and message and allow your consumers agency over the attention they give you. Take the example of the US-based medical devices and healthcare multinational Abbott Laboratories. In their "dignity" campaign, Abbott was lauded for reaching out to consumers who had not yet experienced their products, introducing technologies such as rapid testing (not only for COVID-19 during the pandemic, but also for concerns like concussions) while respecting their customers' sense of agency, in keeping with their maxim that everyone should enjoy the "freedom to live life liberated from the worry and weight of sickness."

Beyond this campaign, Abbott also signals their commitment to agency more broadly. For example, on their website, they expand on this idea, noting that "when people think about health and human dignity, the focus is often on aging or severe illness. To us, it's bigger . . . it's the right to regain your self-reliance, freedom and confidence with your health. To be respected and treated fairly. To be seen as an individual and get the care you require in return. Everyone deserves it." We fully agree.[26]

Even in cases where specific campaigns may not be designed around dignity, we would propose that your pre-consumption consumer's agency can be maintained, or even boosted, in ways that affirm their dignity.

To this end, ask yourself the following questions. If you don't know the answers, we encourage you to ask your customers directly. They'll know, and they'll be pleased to tell you:

- Are your advertising and action triggers transparent in their intent?
- Do you allow consumers to redirect their attention or behavioral intention with dignity?
- Does your advertising credibly communicate that your product offers enlarged, rather than restricted, consumer agency?

Equality at the Pre-Consumption Phase

The third lever in our Marketplace Dignity Framework is equality. Remember that equality happens when people feel that they are treated fairly and they are given the same opportunities to access the value in a good or service as others who are similarly situated.

During the pre-consumption phase of your customers' journey, you can affirm equality by using messages that connect them to goods that offer them actual value, or by placing these goods or products in places where they might be purchased. Now, in the age of mass-media advertising, this might seem intuitive. Isn't equality automatically built in for whoever can access the channels that carry our advertisements? Isn't online mass media open to all, after all?

In reality, firms often design messages and make access decisions that align with what they—not their customers—might prefer. In so doing, they create unequal access, often limiting access for those with the greatest need.

For example, during the COVID-19 pandemic, advertising and communications were critical for both building public health and ensuring that individuals were aware of services and products that may help them stay healthy. But because of stay-at-home and lockdown measures, the bulk of all communications by public health service providers had to shift online—critical and often complex information that was accessible only to those with Wi-Fi or internet access, or with the educational or linguistic resources to make use of it. As a result, the most vulnerable had the least access to these messages and services.[27]

Other challenges to equal access in the pre-consumption phase may be psychological rather than physical or cognitive. Here, the choices we make in representation may doubly affirm or deny dignity. For example, a firm that shows only female children playing with dolls may undermine dignity in two ways: First, they fail to represent their full consumer base, thus failing to see or hear the voices of those who matter for their business. Second, they also create a psychological barrier to learning about or accessing the product at all.[28]

In their research, the UBC Sauder School of Business academics Katherine White and Darren Dahl demonstrate the power of pre-consumption messaging and equality. One anecdote they share showed that simply labeling a steak "Ladies' cut" nudged male consumers away from choosing it, even if a smaller cut was precisely what they wanted.[29]

When we do not prioritize treating all customers equally, the danger is that we push them toward other goods or service providers who may seem more approachable and accessible. And this may not always be the best way to help them meet their goals.

Frederick S. Wherry, Kristin S. Seefeldt, and Anthony S. Alvarez's excellent book *Credit Where It's Due: Rethinking Financial Citizenship* offers this fascinating insight: Many people in underserved communities access pawnbrokers and payday lenders rather than mainstream banks, even though the former often exact high interest rates or are exploitative. This is not because these households don't recognize that the mainstream banks may offer them better outcomes. Rather, it's because many mainstream banks have not invested in making their services equally accessible—geographically, technologically, or practically.[30]

There's an important point to make here: When banks, businesses, or any type of organization fail to affirm equality of access, it's not always or necessarily because of ill intent. Rather, we simply fail to pay enough attention to the way that introductory experiences and initial access to a product need to be designed if we care about centering on dignity. And there are many instances of banks and other institutions doing the right thing in terms of equality, albeit late. In 2020, a Chase bank opened in a historically Black community in the Cherry Hill neighborhood of Baltimore in the United States. It was the first national bank to do so. Here's what Michael Middleton, who leads the nonprofit Cherry Hill Development Corporation, had to say about it: "We've never had any type of financial institution in this community. It says something about a community when you have a bank, a credit union, a financial institution. It says that you are, in a sense, a community that's worthy."[31]

Equal access can also involve the physical entryways to our retail and online spaces. In the UK, studies have shown that hospital design often undermines dignity in precisely this way, presenting spaces that are difficult to navigate, particularly for those experiencing mental or physical impairment. As a result, an estimated 6.9 million outpatient hospital appointments are missed each year. Web interfaces that can't be modified to offer the same access to people with visual impairments or different levels of technological resource availability are the online analog. And if some consumers feel that you have not designed this initial virtual or brick-and-mortar entryway in a way that makes them as welcome as others, you have already denied their dignity in a very real way.[32]

Fortunately, there are simple steps that you can take to create both adaptive and responsive designs. Again, a lot of this hinges on asking yourself a few questions. Let's say you have a website built on rich visuals, complex interactions, and immersive audio experiences. Have you asked yourself whether customers who don't have the latest or largest devices can access your offerings? Could there be better ways to design forms so they are equally easy to complete and submit on all devices?

Equal access can also be as simple as ensuring that you offer multiple languages for audiences with limited English proficiency (who currently represent 8% of the American population) and content that is tailored for audiences including older customers or those with disabilities.[33] And there are plenty of other things that firms can do, depending on your value proposition and positioning.

If your services or products carry certain eligibility criteria, be up front about that and state why. Similarly, if they are universally accessible, make that known in a way that is equally clear. Firms that position themselves in terms of partnership or cocreation with customers can also affirm dignity by directly addressing power differentials that may exist between customer and firm. And this is really key, because equality becomes particularly important when customers and firms hold vastly different amounts of power.

Engaging customers as equal partners can emphasize the inherent value and importance of people, showing that the firm is doing more than using them as a means to an end. An archetypal example of the kind of loyalty that can be engendered by placing an organization on (quite literally) an equal footing with customers is provided by the Green Bay Packers football team. The team is officially owned by a nonprofit, but real control is vested in approximately 540,000 stockholder-fans. A single stockholder is allowed to hold no more than 200,000 shares, which amounts to about 4%. And what's more remarkable is that these shares are accessibly priced.[34]

While direct customer ownership may not be feasible for all firms, inviting customers to be stewards of a brand, recognizing their power in the organization's well-being, and highlighting that even the first-time customer matters are all ways to emphasize the worth of each person with whom your firm interacts.

To make sure that you're designing promotions or campaigns that affirm customers' equal value—to one another and to your organization—consider the following questions:

- Who is the default audience of your communication? Is your advertising content clearly understood by different groups, including different ethnicities? Is it tailored to older consumers, people with disabilities, and other groups that are not in the default population?

- Are you creating introductory or access experiences that are equally physically, culturally, and socially sensitive to the needs of all customers?
- Have you considered adaptive and responsive design in your online channels?
- How might you be able to offer customers a sense of ownership in your firm, product, or service?

In some ways, advertising seems like the easiest part of the consumer journey to get right. But as we hope we've convinced you, it's more complex than it might seem. At the same time, there are a huge number of things you can do to get it, at least, *more* right than you may be at present.

Whether you do one or ten of these things, understanding the extent to which your firm currently affirms or fails to affirm the dignity of customers at the beginning of your journey is a first and critical step. If you do it well, you're likely to enjoy a longer journey alongside them.

Now let's explore the second phase of your customer journey through the lens of our Marketplace Dignity Framework: evaluation.

Chapter 2: Key Insights and Takeaways

- Dignity matters to your customers at the pre-consumption phase: segmenting, advertising, offering promotions, and access.
- Use the three levers of our Marketplace Dignity Framework to ensure you get dignity right from the start: representation, agency, and equality.
- Representation: Acknowledge your customers' strengths (not their weaknesses), strive to tell everyone's story, and personalize campaigns through empowerment not stigmatization.

- Agency: Be transparent about your intentions in advertising, and afford your customers the choice to engage with your campaigns—or not.
- Equality: Ensure that your advertising is inclusive and sensitive to all your customers in ways that empower everyone.

Chapter 3

Marketplace Dignity at the Evaluation Phase
Offering Choice with Respect

In chapter 1, you will remember that we shared an example of Burger King getting marketplace dignity right. Back in 1974, the chain introduced the slogan "Have it your way."

"Have it your way" was conceived to differentiate Burger King's products from those of its main rival, McDonald's. And it was clever. At that time, McDonald's burgers were comparatively limited in range. "Have it your way" was Burger King's way of telling consumers that they had more choice—unlimited choice, was the suggestion—in their restaurants. It also spoke to consumers' sense of individuality, to their desire for control and *agency*. Not only that, it told the customer that what they wanted truly mattered. "We may be King," the ad insisted, "but you, my friend, are the almighty ruler."[1]

Although the firm would go on to experiment with other campaigns, none would resonate as deeply, leading Burger King to reembrace this slogan forty years later. "Having it your way" was the rule, not the exception, at Burger King for decades.

But in 2014, the company had a change of heart. Overnight, a new slogan appeared, this time inviting customers to "Be your way" instead. Self-expression was the thing, said this new ad. And it was our "differences that make us individuals instead of robots."

The campaign landed with less of a bang than a dull thud. *New York Post* columnist John Crudele offered his ill-tempered judgment: "Nah! It just doesn't work."[2] The public seemed to agree—revenue barely inched up 2014–2015 and remained at modern lows right up until 2018.[3] A few years later, the Burger King marketing department had moved on again, this time to "Reclaim the Flame."

"Be your way" affirmed customers' individuality, perhaps. But where "Have it your way" celebrated consumers' agency—their ability to dynamically choose, customize, and design—this was a message about differences that felt generalized, flat, and toned down. Where Burger King previously zeroed in on evaluation and choice as tools of empowerment, now the company offered homilies about self-expression and the human condition. The new slogan came over as platitudinous, something that any brand could say about itself and its products, and with equal accuracy. McDonald's, after all, could just as easily affirm that people had the right to eat what they liked without criticism—indeed, their "You Deserve a Break Today" slogan had done so for decades as well. Burger King had diluted its customers' ability to choose—their agency—and thus failed to assert marketplace dignity as powerfully as before.

The good news, however, is that when your customer has moved through the purchase funnel, from pre-consumption to evaluation and choice, there *are* plenty of things that you can do to optimize marketplace dignity in ways that truly differentiate your brand.

In this chapter, we will explore how to do these things purposefully and with sensitivity to your customers' needs for representation and voice—how to optimize the evaluation and choice experience for them. We will look at ways to empower all your customers to express their identities by providing equitable access and enhancing their agency to evaluate and choose.

Here, we'll argue the case not for increasing choice per se, but for thinking about how you can enrich the potential value of every choice your customer makes. And to help build this case, we'll look at some of the latest research, we'll share feedback from our own surveys, and we'll explore some of the companies that we think do a good job of affirming marketplace dignity in the evaluation and choice phase of their customer journey—and some that do not.

As before, we'll look at all of this through the lens of our Marketplace Dignity Framework.

Representation at the Evaluation and Choice Phase

Representation happens when firms integrate their customers' needs, their concerns, and their voice within the selection of goods and services they offer.

You can do this in two ways. First, you can ensure that customers have a voice in their own evaluation and choice experiences. And second, you can be purposeful about making the experience of selecting the goods and services you offer as inclusive as possible.

Take the story of Tupperware's Brownie Wise. Wise was hired by the iconic homeware brand in the late 1940s, just after the end of World War II, and she struck upon a new idea. Listening to concerns and aspirations—the voices—of the women in her target segment, she quickly gathered that plastic as a material was new and unfamiliar to them. She figured a better approach to having her customers discover Tupperware in the impersonal environment of the department store was to introduce this new product somewhere that felt safe, comfortable, familiar, and socially reinforcing. By the early 1950s, the Tupperware party was thriving: an evaluation and choice experience uniquely tailored to Wise's target segment, and one that presented them with a wide range of choices within the same brand in the comfort of their own homes. Tupperware's sales soared in the 1950s, and the Tupperware party became a thing of lore in its own right.[4]

More recently, another iconic retailer has found its own novel way to give its customers greater representation in the way they evaluate and choose goods. Touted as "an introvert's dream" by *HuffPost*, the beauty giant Sephora's color-coded shopping baskets offer consumers an unobtrusive means of giving voice to their wants and needs. It works like this: A red basket tells sales associates that the customer would like help—the high-touch, expensive, hands-on advice that is critical for many cosmetic customers. But when the customer chooses a black basket, they send a clear message that they want to shop and choose on their own. Not only does this inherently affirm customers' dignity by allowing them to be seen or not, it also optimizes the value of Sephora employees' attention and expertise.[5]

When people feel seen and heard (or are allowed not to be seen and heard), it affirms their dignity. Naturally, when the opposite happens, it's a denial of their dignity. Here's what a twenty-six-year-old female respondent to one of our 2021 consumer surveys told us:

> I was in an Ulta Beauty store. It is a large store, and I needed some guidance on what products would be best for my needs. Every time I have been in this store in the past, several people would come up and ask if I needed assistance. This time no one came. I assumed they were just busy, so I went looking for help. I ended up going to the front counter where several workers were socially chatting. They looked at me standing there obviously wanting help and they ignored me. I stood there for a minute or two feeling awkward before I finally said: "Excuse me, I was hoping someone could help me." One of them peeled off from the group somewhat reluctantly to help me. I felt really bad when standing there. Like I wasn't worthy of their attention. Next time I won't wait so patiently for help, or not go to the store again.[6]

If businesses don't deliberately design the "we won't disturb you" kind of approach that Sephora does, many consumers, particularly marginalized ones, are likely to mistake privacy for lack of attention. Have you ever been in this situation as a customer? Compare that anecdote with this one, also from a 2021 consumer survey: "As a person who purchases plus-sized clothes, Old Navy has always made me feel welcome and respected. I see myself reflected in the employees and love that they have each item that they offer in the Women's Section in all sizes. It's been especially nice to shop at Old Navy now that they have combined their Women's Sections into one as opposed to having the Plus Sized Clothes in a different part of the store."[7]

In this example, the way the store itself is organized can either affirm or deny dignity. Without changing its actual selection, Old Navy simply placed products meeting one set of customers' needs alongside those representing another's. The message they send is that both sets of customers deserve equal representation. In this anecdote, Old Navy ticks the representation and the equality boxes in marketplace dignity. And they do this early in the funnel—during evaluation and choice—at a moment that clearly leaves an impression on the customer.

Of course, in some sectors of the marketplace, full representation and selection integration may not be so easy to achieve. Luxury brands, for instance, often stock a small number of sizes or varieties of a product in-store or do not facilitate easy handling for all customers—given the cost and uniqueness of true luxury and haute couture pieces, preordering all sizes can undermine their business model, and easy access could lead to product damage. For such retailers, investing in technology that makes simulated evaluation easy for a wide range of consumers offers a way of affirming representation in evaluation and choice, while also excelling at the type of highly customized, modern experience that can help time-honored brands remain up to date.

The Swiss luxury watch brand Baume, for example, offers customers the opportunity to use a three-dimensional (3D) configurator on their website. This process is augmented by the opportunity to place a paper wristband on their own arms, mimicking physical engagement. The high quality of the 3D rendering makes this an experience that is perfectly fluid and highly user friendly. And Baume isn't the only one doing this. Makeup brands like Guerlain and MAC are also using virtual try-on technology to provide their customers discretion and privacy (to allow them not to be seen) while enhancing their ability to choose. The result? Around 40% of customers are willing to convert and even spend more on these products, while 70% reportedly feel greater loyalty and engagement to these brands.[8]

And it's not just retail—or even buying and selling, for that matter. Organizations can find manifold ways to ensure that people they work for and with feel seen and recognized. People may in turn be more altruistic toward others.[9]

Intrigued by this, Cait ran an experiment involving a simulated tax payment system to see how greater representation—and agency—would play out in evaluation and choice. In this research, participants came to the lab and completed a task for $10. However, there was a catch. From this $10, participants would need to leave behind a $3 "lab tax" in an envelope on their workstation. Before doing this, some participants got to check a few boxes to indicate what they thought should be done with a portion of the lab tax money collected: how much should go for refreshments for participants, upgraded equipment, or larger bonuses, for example? After they left, Cait and her colleagues matched the envelope to each participant to see who had complied with the $3 requirement. Here's what she found: By simply allowing people to express their preferences—by giving them voice (and agency)—a majority of participants had indeed paid their tax. There must surely be implications there for the federal and other governments in the United States looking to address chronic underpayment of income taxes! And indeed, interesting experiments with this kind of participatory budgeting have been conducted around the world, starting in Porto Alegre, Brazil, with a recent exercise in New York City.[10]

Ensuring that people feel represented and their voices are heard and recognized can and does affirm marketplace dignity at the evaluation and choice phase of their journey with you. And that can have a tremendous impact on how they engage with you, how they feel about your organization, and whether they decide to take the next step of purchasing or consuming (or paying their taxes).

To see how you fare in terms of representing your customers and affirming their dignity in this way when they're evaluating you and your brand, ask yourself these questions:

- Do you actively seek out customer voice and opportunities to recognize the needs of customers when creating your product selections? Are there ways in which you could offer more input in this process?

What Can We Learn About Dignity from a Store that Sells Whoopee Cushions? An Interview with Spencer's CEO, Steven Silverstein

On entering a Spencer's store,[11] you encounter a huge range of products—body jewelry; ironic T-shirts and hats; gag gifts and magic tricks; tarot cards; and an array of intriguing, brightly colored, and titillating intimate items. Especially during the "retail pandemic" of 2020, it might be surprising to some that Spencer's business boomed, far outpacing the growth of competitors.

We'd argue that part of the secret to this success lies in Spencer's deep commitment to affirming their customers' dignity—a commitment that resonated with customers during a time when COVID-19 deprived many people of their sense of freedom and opportunity for self-expression. We spoke with CEO Steven Silverstein, who offered us a glimpse into a number of object lessons in designing for dignity—as well as questions that we should ask if we want to radically respect our customers and thrive while doing so.

The first aspect of dignity that Spencer's nails is representation: both seeing and hearing their customers as they are. To this end, employees are "party hosts," and customers are the guests—welcomed, accepted, and celebrated.

Spencer's dignity design plays out in that surprising, eclectic product assortment itself. By offering products that offer self-expression to a huge range of their customers—resisting the pattern followed by many mall retailers to double down on homogenizing licensing or trend-chasing, Spencer's offers their customers real choice, with no judgment. According to Silverstein, "That's part of the culture here. When the kid is buying fake dog poop, he thinks that's the funniest thing in the world. From an external viewpoint, you can be judgmental—but we don't. And that lets us be us." He adds, "We accept everyone for who they are. And you'll hear this statement among our associates and from our customers: I love Spencer's because I can be who I am."

The reason that this works at Spencer's is because it's literally in the firm's DNA—the business model: As Silverstein says, "We're not a public company—so we don't have to satisfy external constituents like parents. That means that we're all about the kids who love the store, not overly concerned with the people who might judge them. That lets us speak in their language—speak to them."

Further, Spencer's shows the importance of consistent brand-building in offering consumers real agency. As Silverstein says, "Part of our ability to be sincere, authentic, and honest also comes from our concern about the greater world. We know we live in a mall—we aren't for every person who might pass by the store. Because we've been here for such a long time, everyone knows we're going to be out on the edge. And because people understand our brand, they can opt in. They can choose to be part of Spencer's. And once they cross the lease line, we accept them—and they can control their experience."

As Silverstein notes, Spencer's was one of the first retailers to celebrate the lesbian, gay, bisexual, transgender, and queer/questioning (LGBTQ) population. "We didn't wait for it to be OK," he notes. "Spencer's can uniquely cross boundaries and lifestyles . . . we live in this etherworld, where there are so many niches, nooks and crannies. We were inclusive before the rest of the world was inclusive."

But more quietly, the retailer does a remarkable job of inviting their customers to be equal partners in shaping their consumption. Rather than censoring the product assortment, the firm has taken the strategic position that the customer can—and should—have the primary say in what they choose. As Silverstein puts it: "We don't censor. In fact, I think censoring defeats authenticity. When you try to hide things in some way, you're not respecting your customer. We want the honesty. We want the real deal."

- Do you allow customers to express their preferences about the service and support they receive while evaluating and choosing products?
- Does the organization of your store signal inclusive and integrated representation? If this would create challenges for your brand or products, can you use technology in ways that facilitate representation and voice during product evaluation?

Agency at the Evaluation and Choice Phase

Before we go any further, let us reiterate what we said at the start of this chapter: Choice is critical. But simply maximizing choice is not the same thing as affirming agency.

Navigating a plethora of choices can be very hard for some consumers. And all of us are prone to choice overload, as we saw in the example of the US healthcare system.

Sheena Iyengar and Mark Lepper produced a landmark study in the 2000s showing that when people are overburdened by too much choice, they simply end up walking away. In their experiment, Iyengar and Lepper had participants choose between six types of jam without a problem. When that number of choices increased to twenty-four, the same people gave up and left without picking any jam. Their research suggests that when people don't approach a decision with well-formed preferences, large selections can create problems. They can make us feel overwhelmed and dissatisfied with our choices, feel regret, and in many cases, abandon our choice-making altogether.[12]

Now, let's be clear about something else. Through the lens of marketplace dignity, helping consumers manage choice overload isn't just about ensuring that they don't abandon their purchase and thus deprive your company of income—important as that is for your company's success. Investing in tools that help people make choices that match their preferences is a matter of affirming human dignity. And if you've read this far, you will know what the benefits of marketplace dignity are and how they accrue.

So what can we do to design evaluation and choice experiences for agency, and with it, dignity? We propose three main tools to affirm agency during evaluation in choice. They are:

1. Store or choice layout that minimizes choice overload and facilitates evaluation
2. Tailored decision support
3. Late-stage off-ramps

Store Layout

As with representation in evaluation and choice, the physical or visual layout of an environment can enhance and support customers' agency during product or service evaluation and choice.

For retail products, a few basic principles of store design can be key here. Think of the way that major international airports force travelers to navigate a busy and promotion-laden duty-free area and to remain in the midst of the retail environment until shortly before their flight. We strongly believe that this constitutes a denial of dignity: Why should travelers be forced to evaluate and choose (or do the work to avoid being lured in) as part of the price of their plane ticket? Giving them an alternative route that doesn't force people into a retail-heavy environment would accomplish two things: lower congestion in the duty-free store; and respect for the desires of those who have no interest in facing the assault of ads, products, and sales attempts.

And what about those travelers who *are* interested in doing some shopping? The first few feet inside a store's entrance is often called the "decompression zone."[13] This is a space that should allow people to transition from an outside world to an environment where they will evaluate and choose products. Placing large displays or positioning aggressive salespeople in this zone may allow a store to drive attention to high-margin goods or control traffic flow, but it doesn't respect the prospective customers' agency in directing their own attention.

Something that stores often get wrong are so-called grid setups, where merchandise is displayed in straight, unbroken rows with little empty space. Here, people do not have the option to skip directly to the products they want to buy. They may bump into one another in crowded aisles, with few options in directing their relationship to other consumers. The lack of white space almost always guarantees overload, and with it a loss of true agency and dignity. The cross-cutting lane that breaks up the long aisles in the typical big supermarket is more important than it first looks.

Thoughtful retailers have come up with dignity-affirming alternatives. One use of decompression space that became popular during the COVID-19 pandemic was to offer customers the option of hand sanitizers and disinfectant wipes, as well as the most up-to-date recommendations for safe shopping. By replacing busy stockpiled displays from the area around entries, retailers empowered customers to take actions that made them feel safe as they evaluated and chose groceries rather than creating immediate pressure to buy something the store was trying to push out the door.

Walmart has also been a leader in supporting customers' agency in shopping. Notably, the redesign of their stores and checkout area in 2022 allows customers to select their own way of checking out: They can work with a cashier, select self-checkout, or choose assisted self-checkout. Not only does this type of redesign allow more unimpeded space (and thus, more control over one's choice experience), it saves resources. More broadly, Walmart's redesign focuses on allowing customers to choose the type of experience they want to have throughout the store. As Alvis Washington, vice president of marketing, store design, innovation, and experience, tells *Fast Company*: "I say we want our store to play a role on a productivity journey, so customers and members save time finding the products they need, so they can spend time on experiences they want."[14]

Tailored Decision Support

What about supporting customer choice-making? In the United States, a national survey revealed that patients facing a healthcare choice wanted to know about the risks of treatment options ahead of them and have healthcare providers listen to their concerns. Decision aids such as the Diabetes Medication Choice Decision Aid, in which patients can choose a treatment that suits their context (type, frequency of testing, method of administration) and then work with their doctors to make side-by-side comparisons of these drugs speak to a need that is acutely felt in the moment of choice.[15]

But medical care is often notoriously low in agency at the point of choice (and especially in terms of costs in the United States), partly because patients simply do not have access to the information they need or time to evaluate multiple options. NBC News reported the experience of Nicole Briggs, who went to the emergency room near her home in Denver and was diagnosed with appendicitis. She rushed to the Swedish Medical Center hospital but called ahead to make sure it took her insurance. When the hospital said yes, Briggs thought that meant she was covered—not just by the hospital, but by the anesthesiologist, surgeon, and nursing staff. Two months after her surgery, she got a bill for $4,727 from the surgeon, and after she declined to pay the bill, the collection agency put a lien on her home. They also ended up garnishing her wages by 25% every month. She was pregnant at the time and didn't think she would be able to afford the cut in her pay.[16]

Other healthcare providers are doing a better job of providing agency in consumer choice, even in the case of lifesaving treatments. Boston Scientific's Watchman product, an implant that is designed to reduce stroke risk, is supported by a phone line that not only connects interested people to medical professionals but also offers connections to "patient ambassadors." These ambassadors are freely available to anyone considering the device and form a community built on firsthand experience. Both prospective and ambassador patients are afforded the dignity of agency in this all-too-critical evaluation and choice process.[17]

Late-Stage Off-Ramps

As customers approach a final decision, the preservation of their agency is critical. Rather than progressively locking customers into a purchase, a more dignity-affirming approach to evaluation and choice provides off-ramps, or ways for consumers to reconsider purchases when checking out.

Think of the times when a customer who has evaluated a good might have felt trapped into taking it home. In the United States, finance options for automobiles are typically suspended until a customer effectively agrees to buy the vehicle. If the financing does not turn out to be favorable or within the customer's budget, the hours spent in the dealership, the effort of the salesperson and finance professionals, and the keys in their hand become strong disincentives to walk away. Once a salesperson has shown us a product, there is often a lot of pressure to buy. Not only does this build on the famous "endowment effect," where we become more attached to things of which we've taken even psychological owner-ship, it makes some strategic sense for firms: We stop the leaks in the purchase funnel. But what we're not doing is affirming market-place dignity.[18]

Unfortunately, designing for agency in evaluation and choice in this problematic way is extremely common. We know of no firm that goes out of its way to offer more, rather than fewer, opportunities to step back from a choice once customers are far into the purchase process. Admittedly, this is a difficult decision for organizations, which have the responsibility to shareholders of revenue growth. But what about longer-term customer loyalty? And the cost of pur-chase cancellations and returns? Wouldn't it make more sense to build engagement and offer the products or services that our custom-ers actually want—even if it means that they end up feeling more empowered to go ahead and abandon the purchase?

When a customer decides they have bought something that they don't actually want or need, most of the time they have the right to send it back. But returns are an extremely expensive business. In 2018 alone, a full 10% of retail purchases were returned in the United States, totaling a whopping $369 billion. That's a lot of money (and very likely lost loyalty) waiting farther down the line.[19]

We would urge you to do the right thing in terms of honoring your customers' agency in the evaluation and choice process of their journey with you. Design your sales outlet (be it bricks and mortar or online) in a way that respects their dignity. Support their decision-making and give them an easy way out if they decide the purchase is not for them at this point. They'll thank you for it.

Ask yourself the following questions:

- Have you consulted consumers about what kinds of physical space, time frames, social contexts, modes of delivery, or even layout of the evaluation and choice environment best support the decisions they want to make?
- If you have captured consumer voice in evaluation and choice, have you created a choice environment that reflects that you have seen their experiences and heard their needs?
- Do you allow customers options for voice, both in *how* they choose and *what* they choose, throughout the decision experience?
- Do you have clear off-ramps for customers throughout their evaluation and choice processes?

Equality at the Evaluation and Choice Phase

All customers should be offered the same range of choices.

The principle sounds simple, doesn't it? However, in practice, equality can be a difficult thing to get right in terms of marketplace dignity. In our work, we've found that there are two things that can help avoid some pitfalls:

- Recognizing the implied *hierarchies* that surface in your selection and distribution decisions
- Spotting bias in access opportunities for customers to evaluate and choose your goods and services

What do we mean by these things?

Let's take a look at the fashion industry again. Historically, in most parts of the world, being thin is seen as fashionable. Customers who wear smaller sizes—particularly women—have been advantaged over others. In this way, the fashion industry has been consistently poor at representing all its customers. But it's also guilty of creating a kind of hierarchy in its consumer base: Slimmer customers are effectively more valuable than others and therefore have access to more choice and selection.[20]

Increasingly, brands are understanding that such choices reinforce types of inequity; they damage self-esteem and stigmatize swaths of the consumer community. One such dignity-affirming brand is Universal Standard, which carries sizes from 00 to 40. Their website reads: "We wanted a size 40 to shop in the same way as a size 00—using style as her only filter."[21]

Such choices to affirm the equal value of all customers can have massive impacts. As a 41-year-old US-based respondent to our 2021 survey relates:

> I was shopping for the first time after having my first child. I'd never had to shop for plus size clothing and I was feeling depressed, angry and just didn't want to do it because I felt ashamed for putting on so much weight and I thought I looked disgusting . . .
>
> The first store I went to exclusively sells to plus size women and she noticed that I had walked all over the store looking at things. She approached me and asked if it was my first time being there. I told her it was and she was just so positive, willing to help and told me women of all sizes are beautiful and deserved to be treated well and spoil themselves with wonderful clothing.
>
> She spent an hour with me picking out a new wardrobe for my new, larger body. I thought differently of myself after the experience.[22]

Salespeople should also recognize the role that they play in ensuring equal access to evaluation opportunities, some of which might be driven by their expectations about what types of customers will look for access to some goods over others. Again, when this works, it is likely to build loyalty of a kind that is otherwise difficult to attain.

As another US-based respondent shared:

> I have a son who is almost 14, and he is really into makeup and beauty products, skin care, and fragrances. He gravitates toward scents that are marketed to women, as he prefers floral scents. We were looking at the various perfumes and gift sets, and spraying samples. A salesperson came to see if we needed any help. I explained that I actually prefer muskier scents, and we were shopping for my son.
>
> I've experienced things like this before, where a salesperson then pulls a quick face of shock and surprise. However, in this case, the salesperson was not bothered one bit and then asked my son if he needed any assistance or wanted any recommendations on scents she likes. It made me feel really great for him, that there are people who won't judge him for what he likes.[23]

Success and failure to affirm equality in evaluation and choice are not just the purview of the fashion and beauty industries. A study found strong, pervasive biases surrounding ethical purchases for people with low incomes who are on government assistance. For example, the researchers found that while people with high incomes were seen as more moral for choosing organic over conventional foods, individuals receiving government assistance were perceived as *less* moral for making an identical choice.[24]

These people were effectively denied the dignity of pursuing the same higher-level needs as more affluent counterparts: to express their values, protect their family's health, or support sustainability. For them, this was seen as morally corrupt, and it could well be part of the reason that lower-income neighborhoods in the United States typically offer fewer healthier food outlets.[25]

Another example of access bias is clear in the availability of feminine hygiene products in Africa. Over the last few years, a growing community of women have expressed their frustration about the lower quality of Always pads in Kenya, citing cases of burning, dermatological reaction, and discomfort. In 2019, the hashtag #My

AlwaysExperience started gaining traction, prompting women to share stories of their frustration. As is often the case in our research, here we see a connection between equality and representation: The sense that Kenyan women were being treated worse than other countries (an experience of inequality) was compounded by initially bland denials by Procter & Gamble (P&G).[26]

And even as the company later claimed to have heard and seen their customers, activists continued to point out that not all women had the agency to upgrade to the premium products designed to meet quality standards that were ubiquitous in the rest of the world. In a nutshell, P&G was effectively depriving Kenyan women of the opportunity to evaluate and choose among their higher-quality products. In the era of social media, such inequity is unlikely to remain a secret; in this case, women took agency, reclaimed their voices, and continued to put pressure on the brand to improve.[27]

The examples we have cited here are by no means unique. In every industry, sector, and geographical location, there are organizations fighting the good fight in respecting the equality of their customers' choices. But any firm can risk denying equality—and marketplace dignity—by failing to provide the same options for all customers, regardless of their financial constraints, socioeconomic status, or the markets they represent.

A good way to guard against this is to ask yourself where you stand in terms of safeguarding equality at this phase in your customer journey. Ask yourself questions like these:

- Does your product selection allow equal opportunities to sample and fully evaluate products across diverse demographic characteristics?
- Are those products designed for higher-level needs (identity, health, and sustainability, say) equally available to consumers facing different levels of financial constraint or of different socioeconomic statuses?
- Are there any ways in which your channel decisions may be creating inequitable options for customers or implying a

hierarchy that elevates some customers' worth at the cost of others'?

And where you find it hard to take concrete steps to affirm marketplace dignity in choice and evaluation, we would urge you at least to identify and recognize the impact.

Think about the loss of actual customers or future value creation—the loss of face suffered by some of the brands mentioned in this chapter. And try to consider the power of affirming representation, agency, and equality in differentiating your brand, bolstering its purpose and encouraging your customers through the funnel toward actual consumption.

Chapter 3: Key Insights and Takeaways

- Dignity matters to your customers at the evaluation and choice phase: at the point of purchase, whether in-store or virtually.
- Use the three levers of our Marketplace Dignity Framework to ensure you get dignity of choice right: representation, agency, and equality.
- Representation: Ensure that customers have a voice in how they want to evaluate and choose, and be purposeful about making the product selection and experience as inclusive as possible.
- Agency: Design your layouts to support how your customers prefer to make their choices; offer tailored decision support; and provide off-ramps or exit points in the purchasing funnel at this phase.
- Equality: Ensure that all your customers enjoy the same access and opportunities to sample your goods and that aspirational or higher-end needs are equitably accommodated.

Chapter 4

Marketplace Dignity at the Consumption Phase
Experiences That Affirm Dignity

So far, we have looked at ways to affirm marketplace dignity in the early phases of pre-consumption and evaluation: how to attract and connect with your customer in ways that honor their identity and their choices before they actively engage with you. And we've looked at a few examples of brands that have gotten this right, and some others, less so. In this chapter, we will look at how you can use the Marketplace Dignity Framework to affirm dignity when your customers make the purchase and experience your products and services.

But first, let us share a case that many of you might remember. Back in 2019, the US-based exercise and media firm Peloton went viral . . . for all the wrong reasons. Some of you may recall that the company released a thirty-second advertisement for its static exercise bike. Titled "The Gift That Gives Back," the spot featured a woman receiving the bike from her partner and making a video diary about her gift, which featured entries such as, "A year ago, I didn't realize how much this would change me."[1]

The backlash was immediate. Social media users inferred a sexist—even "dystopian"—subtext, with hidden messages about female physique and a need to conform to certain body types to please (male) partners. Spoofed by comedians, derided by the press, and quickly converted into a host of internet "memes," the advertisement was an out-and-out public relations disaster, one that coincided with a 9% drop in the value of Peloton stock.[2]

Yet behind the scenes, another story was unfolding. Peloton users, *actual customers* who had purchased the bike and subscribed to its interactive fitness services, had expressed nothing but praise for the product and the company. This customer base in fact spoke enthusiastically about the representation, agency, and equality inherent in the Peloton experience: an experience that empowered them with choice of the types of workouts they wanted, regardless of their physical condition or ability.[3]

And Peloton instructors, a multinational cohort of trained fitness teachers paid by the company to lead different types of rides, were also vocal in their support of the brand. Cait is a Peloton enthusiast and loves what one of the fitness teachers, Sam Yo, had to say about the experience that the company offered its users: "In this crowd, you are never lost. You're always seen. You're always heard, no matter who you are."

Not only does the Peloton bike interface allow users to be both seen on a leaderboard or not seen (they can choose to ride without participation on the leaderboard) and to be heard via "high fives," the product's design also emphasizes choice, giving customers many class options as well as the opportunity to ride outside of a formal class, and ensures fairness. Riders completing their 500th ride are not treated any differently than those who have completed their 10th.

And the numbers speak for themselves. Peloton weathered the "Gift That Gives Back" imbroglio with aplomb. By 2020, sales had doubled. Of course, this may have something to do with COVID lockdowns and stay-at-home orders, but it's important to note that Peloton actually reduced the cost of their bike by 16% to help customers budget better during the pandemic.[4]

The case of Peloton is curious. On the one hand, here is a brand caught up in controversy surrounding representation at the phase. On the other, the organization had designed a consumption experience that inspired brand loyalty that grew their customer base at an average rate of 10% year over year.[5]

This is true of almost any brand—they can get dignity right at one stage while making a mistake at another. It is also true that "The Gift That Gives Back" had its share of shortcomings. But at the experience stage, Peloton offered their customers and trainer associates a consumption experience that emphasized inclusivity (i.e., being both interactive and representative) and permitted individuals to select the program that worked best for them. Given this, it's not hard to see why Peloton had generated so much loyalty despite some missteps.

Now let's take a look at how you can ensure that your products and services are designed to affirm dignity as a function of consumer experience using our Marketplace Dignity Framework. And on the way, we'll share some examples of other firms, organizations, and sectors that have hit—and missed—the mark.

Representation at the Consumption Phase

Getting your customer to convert can feel, in itself, like a milestone. As you make your sale and calculate new revenue, it can be tempting to stop worrying quite so much about marketplace dignity. But that would be a mistake.

At the consumption phase, you have a unique opportunity to gauge whether you got it right or wrong when you were figuring out the design of your product or service. And to channel that learning back into building customer loyalty and opening up new markets for your brand. Representation is key here. Take smartphones.

Connected, handheld devices have essentially democratized access to information, communication, connection with others, and the ability to document life events for people all over the world. From the most privileged to those struggling the most, the iPhone and its competitors can claim with some accuracy that they represent all their customers. But not always: For years, people with darker skin tones have been underrepresented by the cameras in their smartphones. No matter how great the boasts about new features and advanced capabilities, most phone cameras left people of color looking washed out in photos or unnaturally dark- or light-skinned.

Google took a stance on this issue with the launch of their Pixel 6 in 2022. Their Super Bowl advertisement, seen by millions of consumers around the world, was called "Seen on Pixel." The ad features a song performed by the Black superstar Lizzo and relates the "story" of Real Tone, a major iteration of the firm's camera and imaging technology and a significant attempt on Google's part to "accurately represent all skin tones."

The spot was accompanied by this message from Google's chief marketing officer (CMO), Lorraine Twohill: "Because everyone deserves to be seen as they truly are, we are committed to addressing this gap. Internally, Googlers of color volunteered to test the camera on Pixel 6 before we launched it and provided input on what was working and what could be better."[6]

Doing this required a significant investment. Google had to work with photographers known for photographs of communities of color. Collectively, they took thousands of photos that they say made their training set twenty-five times more diverse.[7] Further, the company invited these photographers and other artists to give feedback on the photos themselves, as part of their efforts to improve the aesthetics of how photos were finished. Representation and equality in everything, said Twohill, should always be "the norm and the default."

At the same time, Google also upgraded voice recognition to identify people with different speech patterns and accents and ensure that the quality of translations is 18% improved over the previous version, allowing people to communicate in their own language much better.[8]

Again, we just want to stress that we believe that marketplace dignity in consumption is, morally, the *right thing to do*. Getting it right in representation of all those customers that pay for your goods and services should, as Twohill says, be the ethical default. But there's also a clear business benefit attached to the marketplace dignity imperative here. We believe that it is no coincidence that Google's

Pixel 6, modified and enhanced to better represent the entirety of its customer base, went on to enjoy sales greater than Pixel 4 and Pixel 5 combined. One report suggests that in the first full quarter following the Pixel 6 launch in 2022, Google's sales growth on Pixel skyrocketed, increasing by around 400% year on year.[9]

But while finding inventive and thoughtful ways to represent the entirety of the customer that consumes your brand is critical, remember that it is just as important to be mindful and represent the right *not* to be seen or recognized, where appropriate. Take the Canada Learning Bond, a government-backed welfare program designed to help families with low incomes cover the costs of their children's education. As well intentioned as the initiative is, the Canada Learning Bond has come under fire from some Canadian researchers who find that the requirement to come into a bank and open an account to receive funds may be stigmatizing for families who are struggling financially. Within its first year of launch, only 16% of eligible families had taken it up.[10] The in-person requirement, says Rotman professor Dilip Soman, essentially dissuaded customers from taking the opportunity to receive $2,000 in aid. Despite qualifying for full access, many families may forgo the aid in part because they do not want to publicly acknowledge that they are in need of this kind of help.

And there are plenty of products that we can think of—products that are conceived to help as many people as possible in as equitable and representative fashion as possible—that still fall short of full representation in the actual consumption phase because they highlight or draw attention to something that some people may not want to share. The hospital gown—the "Johnny"—is a good example. These flimsy, insubstantial, open-backed garments are offered to patients in all kinds of healthcare settings. For healthcare providers, they work well: the Johnny is cheap to manufacture at scale, and for practitioners and patients, it has the advantage of being easy to remove. But in terms of design, the Johnny does a poor job of respecting the right to be seen—or not—in a way that fully affirms every patient's dignity. This is probably because healthcare systems have failed to include actual users in designing the garment. The Johnny was put together without there being a patient in the room.[11] As a result, says Dr. Bridget Duffy, the chief medical officer of Vocera, "the first thing hospitals do is strip patients of their dignity."[12]

Interestingly, several US healthcare providers have begun to explore ways of making their gown designs more aligned with patient interests. One well-known provider, the Cleveland Clinic, has gone so far as to hire high-end fashion designer Diane von Furstenberg to create a model that mimics her own brand's exclusive clothing line, offering ways to provide easy access for clinicians while preserving patient privacy. Another, the Henry Ford Health System, has part-nered with utility clothing maker Carhartt to create a garment that would better resonate with patients in the Detroit area, launching the Model D hospital gown in 2015.[13] Meanwhile, the scrubs manufac-turer Care+Wear has created a front-tying, pocketed kimono-style gown line to offer patients greater modesty while also maintaining desired utility and function.[14]

However, none of these innovations have fully taken off in any truly disruptive sense. And the reason is likely to do with costs. Designing and manufacturing a von Furstenberg hospital gown constitutes an expensive alternative to a simple, paper-based, back-less garment.[15] And for healthcare providers around the world—particularly public services that may already be grappling with high or even increasing financial burdens—they are just too costly to consider. The takeaway? Representation needs to be financially viable. These one-off projects by famous designers show that a bet-ter way is possible, but the challenge will be for someone to make this happen at scale, across many more hospitals, and at the right price point.

Being physically seen (or not) is one thing. But in the consump-tion phase of your customer journey, privacy in a more general sense must be a critical consideration as you think about representation. As we discussed earlier in this book, in our always-on, digitized, and connected world, recognizing and respecting your customer's pri-vacy are fundamental requirements.

Femtech is a sector increasingly under scrutiny from the press and media for failing to fully affirm the dignity and the privacy of its active users. In recent years, more than $1 billion has been invested in the so-called femtech sector. Apps that track and predict women's menstrual cycles and fertility have boomed since the mid-2010s. But just as these apps have proliferated in the market (reports suggest that there are more than 200 femtech companies, with millions of users worldwide), serious concerns are emerging about the use of data that they collect from users.

While proponents talk about femtech as a tool for female empowerment, the sector is also courting a certain amount of controversy. A 2018 investigation by the US news and opinion website Vox was scathing in its criticism of "menstrual tracking," concluding that period-trackers were not only largely inaccurate, but they also actively denied the dignity of women. The piece cites one user whose app would not "allow" her to track her menstrual cycle. There were ingrained assumptions in the app, which were not "just a matter of having a few extra annoying boxes on the in-app calendar that one can easily ignore [but] yet another example of technology telling queer, unpartnered, infertile, and/or women uninterested in procreating that they aren't even women," the user reported.[16]

One 2023 CNN report (among many others) highlights some poorly understood, and so far ill-defined, areas of US law, where app designers such as Femm, Flo, Ovia Health, and Clue could be required to give user data to law enforcement services in US states where abortion has been criminalized—this in the wake of the US Supreme Court's overturning of *Roe v. Wade* in 2022.[17]

And according to Statista, a data company, this problem could well be set to balloon. They report that "over 90% of the apps required sensitive data that directly identifies the person. Furthermore, around 50% of the apps evaluated collected data when the app was in use."[18]

Then there's the thorny issue of companies monetizing customer consumption information. The pharmacy giant Walgreens went viral on Twitter after it "sold" customer data to a third party in 2022. One customer, "Nicole," congratulated the company after she received a package of Enfamil infant formula and pacifiers after purchasing a pregnancy test. The tweet read: "Dear Walgreens, I received this package today a week after purchasing a pregnancy test at your store. I was asked to take the test by my doctor despite having no Fallopian tubes. 1/X." It was liked by nearly 170,000 Twitter users and retweeted more than 31,000 times.[19]

When you share the consumption data of your customers, you risk denying them their marketplace dignity, especially if doing so results in them receiving products or services that are misaligned with their actual needs or wants. A key consideration then is: Which of your goods, services, or practices require you to *expose* your customers in ways that might make them feel just as undignified as they might in a flapping hospital gown? And there could be any number of these. For instance, your website might force users to accept cookies if they want to access your content—and thereby agree to more exposure than makes them comfortable. In your restaurant or bar, food orders might be yelled to kitchen staff, inadvertently spotlighting a diner's indulgent choices. Your hair or nail salon might feature glass windows that invite passersby to scrutinize your clients—one of us has squirmed through a foil-wrapped experience like this in the past. From major to minor, from the "intimate surveillance" of mobile apps to simple but careless choices about how your customer consumes your products and services, you might be failing to represent all their needs and, worse, their rights. And in doing so, you erode their enjoyment, satisfaction, and inevitably, future loyalty to you and your brand.

So how can you help guard against this? When your customers are at the consumption phase of their journey with you, prioritize representation. Ask yourself the following three questions. And if the answer to any of these questions is no, then ask yourself what you can do about it:

- Are all our customers equally capable of engaging fully with our product or service?

- Has product design, service, or technical testing been carried out in ways that assess performance against the characteristics and needs of *all* our consumers?
- Do people have the ability to consume our products or services privately if they choose to do so?

Agency at the Consumption Phase

Let's turn now to the second lever of the Marketplace Dignity Framework. Remember that we talk about agency in terms of how empowered your customers are and their ability to choose what they want. In the consumption phase of their journey with you—once they have made a purchase—your customers become the owners of the experience you are selling.

Think about that for a second. Once someone has made the decision to buy what you are selling, they are now in a position to decide when, how, and with whom to experience the service or product you are selling them.

That sounds simple enough on paper. And in theory, building agency into the consumption experience shouldn't be hard. Giving your customer control and choice can be readily built into anything you offer. Nor is it hard to ensure that they are aware of their own agency. When we conduct field research, for instance, we typically remind respondents that they have control over the way a survey flow proceeds. Their feedback confirms that this affirms their feelings around dignity.

So how do *you* know that your customer feels agency in their experience with *you*? A first step is to simply stop and ask yourself some questions at each touch point. Are you making consumers' agency clear? Do they know what they can choose? If you can offer and deliver different consumption options without incurring massive costs, are you happy to do so?

Of course, you might argue that not all products and services are the same. Some are clearer cut than others: giving customers a choice of apparel to buy, a destination to fly to and the choice of airline seat that meets their preferences and budget, a range of insurance packages to choose, or subscription packages that map to different needs or schedules. Here, agency in consumption feels clear.

But what about experiences that involve the direct expertise of a practitioner? Healthcare interventions, say? What does agency matter if you are a patient going into an operating room? Doesn't it make more sense to hand agency over to your surgeon or consultant?

Healthcare is an interesting paradigm. For patients and their loved ones, lack of agency—feelings of real powerlessness—constitute a genuine problem. A recent study noted that, particularly for older adults suffering chronic conditions, powerlessness, anger, frustration, and with it, nonadherence to physician recommendations, were common experiences. Attempts to correct such experiences via simple information provision, interestingly, are inconclusive at best in their outcomes.[20]

In response, we would argue that informational interventions often fall flat because they fail to affirm patient dignity. Think about it. A deluge of to-dos can be overwhelming. Remember what we said about choice in chapter 1? Presenting customers, be they patients or others, with an *overload* of information or choice can just as easily rob them of their agency as withholding options from them.

Small things can help here. In the healthcare context, couldn't patient agency be affirmed by putting easy, simplified questions to individuals during the pre-op process: writing down questions on a board in the waiting room so patients can think of answers, printing them on a form, and sending simple text messages that have been shown to drive a sense of power and control, and in turn the dignity of patients awaiting intervention?

For example, a preset board in the preoperative space might include the following:

- What name do you want us to use for you when you are under anesthesia?

- How do you want us to communicate with your loved ones about your procedure?
- What do you need in order to feel ready to begin?

Whatever your organization or line of business, how might these kinds of simple, low-cost interventions work for your customers? Can you think of any examples?

The golden rule here is to avoid overburdening your customers. Apple famously began as a company that, by simplifying its design, gave consumers agency over their experience. Gone were the days of excessive remote controls and multibutton devices. Rather, a simple thumb-touch could advance, rewind, and turn the volume of your music up or down.

Fast-forward a decade or two. The complexity of Apple products has become a notorious source of frustration for many customers. Many users complain of feeling powerless or under-resourced in terms of managing their Apple product or service. Repairing a broken iPhone typically requires an appointment at the Genius Bar—a name truly designed to rob nongenius consumers of their agency, if ever there was one. Getting this appointment is not easy. First, the customer must access the Apple website. Then the customer has to commit to a preset appointment. Alternatively, customers have to wait in line until an Apple Genius is free.[21]

Further, Apple products can speak easily only to other Apple products, creating multiproduct lock-in that reduces consumer agency across many categories. If you want to buy via an Apple device, you pay the way that Apple wants you to pay. There is no more mix-and-match. Apple has you, and you break ranks at your own risk.

In response, the Authority for Consumers and Markets in the Netherlands informed Apple in 2021 that their control of payment mode in the App Store was anticompetitive. The European Union has raised similar concerns. These cases are likely to wend their way through the courts very slowly, giving Apple customers plenty of time to continue feeling a loss of control, ownership, and agency.

The top brass at Apple might do well to heed this post, recently shared on the Free Software Foundation's community page: "Threatening danger, fraud, or malware are all clever and often used ways of scaring users into agreeing to ever more restricting user terms and conditions. The cost of developing ways to keep users safe is not about finances, but power . . . And make no mistake, despite misleading advertising, there is also no freedom for users in the way Apple runs its App Store. We must remember that having freedom is not 'insecure,' rather, it is a precondition for true privacy."[22]

In theory, building agency into the customer consumption experience should be easy. In practice, there are pitfalls. And depending on the type of organization or sector you inhabit, these can be more or less pernicious. Some of our collective research looks at the consumption experience with government agencies, for instance. In this context, interactions typically integrate less consumer agency than in the consumer goods marketplace. A customer who is dissatisfied with the performance of a new car can return the vehicle to the dealership under most countries' laws and decide to buy another type of car. But the same customer who is dissatisfied with the Department of Motor Vehicles cannot simply choose another driver's license provider. Similarly, to the chagrin of millions of Americans, tax payment in the United States is not voluntary, and many citizens report feeling quite helpless in their interactions with the Internal Revenue Service (IRS).[23]

To make matters worse, we have found that in these low-agency environments, customers' feelings of representation (being seen and heard) and equality of treatment fare poorly too. In one of our surveys around dignity affirmation experience with government bodies, a respondent told us: "I felt respected by the government when I finally received my tax return from 2020. It took way longer than it usually does. I was waiting and waiting for months. I completed my return in February. I did not receive it until May. It was very frustrating and stressful. My family was needing that return. I felt at ease. I responded with happiness. I felt like I could relax after receiving my refund."[24] It's easy to see how this experience, which ended well here, could have been made much better if dignity had been affirmed in the process.

Another survey response reveals how much representation, voice, and equity matter, even when agency itself is in short order:

> My dignity was respected when there was an issue with one of my tax returns. I called the IRS because I could see that a mistake was made on their end. I was on the telephone with an IRS agent for over an hour until the problem was resolved. I was treated with dignity and respect on the phone call. The IRS agent apologized to me every time that she had to put me on hold to do more research on the problem or talk to a supervisor. She said she was sorry that it was taking so much time and because the error was obviously on their end. She treated me with dignity and apologized for the time I needed to spend to address their error. Because she treated me this way, I was patient and treated her with dignity as well. I felt respected and treated her with respect.[25]

In this section, we have focused largely on healthcare and government agencies and have shared the example of Apple. Regardless of your organization, sector, or market, we believe that there are several key takeaways for you and your business. When designing for agency in the consumption experience of your customers, be sure to ask yourself the following three questions:

- Do you know if your existing customers feel in control of the experience? Do they know they have choices, and have you ensured that their agency is optimized and communicated at different touch points?
- In cases where expert or firm control is desirable, do you empower consumers to shape the aspects of their experience in which *they* are the experts?
- If you can't provide agency, can you compensate for that by making sure that people feel seen and heard (i.e., representation

is strong) and are aware that they are being fairly treated (i.e., equality is reinforced)?

Equality at the Consumption Phase

One of the big ideas about our modern world, particularly in the wake of the pandemic, is that technology has become a *great equalizer.*

At the start of this chapter, we congratulated Google for doing its part to better represent smartphone camera users of all colors and races—and for correcting a historical inequity in this sense. Yet, for all their imperfections, technologies like handheld devices and communication apps certainly have a role to play in democratizing human beings' access to information, to each other, and to opportunities to share and contribute—regardless of very many of the indicators of inequality.

The popularity of TikTok in a number of small towns and villages of India is a great example. TikTok is a short-form video-hosting service owned by the Chinese internet giant ByteDance. The app does not require fluency in English to operate and works well even over low-speed internet. As stay-at-home mother Mamta Verma, who lives in a small town in Madhya Pradesh, India, told Al Jazeera, Instagram and YouTube are for "the big people." She felt comfortable using TikTok, however, probably because she felt equal as a user and included in the opportunity to share and experience things with other people: "Before TikTok, I didn't have the confidence to talk to people. I would just do my work."[26] For the first time, here was a digital space that rural India was enjoying, said the same article.

Those of us who have recently lived large portions of our lives on WhatsApp, Messenger, Snapchat, or any other social media app can relate. And in the workplace, communications apps have been steadily broadening equitable access as the shift to remote work gathers momentum. Some of the biggest players have made laudable efforts in driving equality here.

Zoom, for instance, defaults to the allocation of equally sized screen space for all participants and reduces the disparities created by positions in a physical room or simple physical size. As a result, it has been dubbed "the great equalizer," making interruption less difficult, prompting broader invitations to previously size-limited meetings, and overcoming socialized tendencies to sit in the back of the room. Even for those who might have previously benefited from their physical stature, this has come as something of a relief.[27]

Reporter Nadya Ellerhorst, who characterizes herself as "vertically gifted," writes that in the 2020 Zoom-heavy experience, she no longer felt she literally stood out, drawing stares and questions about a supposed proclivity for basketball. She writes: "Instead, there is just me, seated at my screen, like everyone else. Even though I am a vehement denier of the overarching concept of 'normal,' I can't help but say that I feel somewhat 'normal' for once. For the first time, I am going about my life without feeling self-conscious or different as a result of my height. Although circumstances revert back to the way they were when I go out for walks, my educational and extracurricular life has taken on a new character, one that is not influenced by my 72 inches."[28]

Zoom, TikTok, and other programs may not be perfect apps or brands. But they deserve praise for driving equality of experience for a majority of online users and customers.

In the physical world of bricks and mortar, many other organizations are being purposeful about delivering equitable experiences for consumers who have purchased their products or services. McDonald's in France has long been doing interesting things here. The fast-food giant has directly targeted diverse communities to execute a strategy for inclusion. The chain has hosted and sponsored different types of events in heterogeneous neighborhoods; installing game tables around high-rise apartment blocks (historically flash points for social unease and crime), sponsoring kids' sporting events, and staging school visits.

Again, McDonald's as a brand has its fair share of detractors, and for diverse reasons. However, in putting its clout behind this kind of activity, the hamburger behemoth has won plaudits—particularly among people who have experienced forms of exclusion within

French society. The Golden Arches—an invitation to consume fast food—is now increasingly being seen as a gateway to nonhierarchical employment, collaboration, training, and opportunity. In French cities in the south, McDonald's employees are known to be fiercely loyal to the brand and to prioritize a culture based around family values as a result.

When one McDonald's restaurant in a marginalized area of Marseilles went into liquidation and legal limbo after the COVID-19 pandemic hit, a group of employees stepped in to avoid its closure. Without even soliciting permission from the chain, they repurposed their beloved McDonald's restaurant building as a food pantry called "L'Après M." Adapting the McDonald's French slogan, "Come as you are," to the statement, "As you are, you come," the store now feeds hundreds of families per week, delivers food to the elderly, and makes sure everyone is treated fairly.[29]

And it's not just France. Across the United States, McDonald's provides the same, equitable context—the bricks-and-mortar setting—that enables millions of Americans to forge and sustain real and valuable connections, regardless of their background or how much (or little) they consume. Chris Arnade, writing in the UK's *Guardian* newspaper, has this to say about the US chain: "McDonald's: You can sneer, but it's the glue that holds communities together."[30] The chain has offered routes to employment, financial success, and community for many Black communities in the United States, as Marcia Chatelain relates in her Pulitzer Prize–winning book *Franchise: The Golden Arches in Black America.*[31]

Physical space can communicate equity in other ways. The US "Commit to Sit" initiative encourages nurses to sit beside patients when talking with them. This equalization of height enhances the degree to which patients feel treated with courtesy and respect, are listened to carefully, and receive clear explanations—all while simultaneously increasing the time that patients feel a nurse had spent with them. Following its launch in 2016, patient satisfaction scores rose from the 9th to the 43rd percentile.[32]

Importantly, these effects emerged only when nurses started asking patients if they could sit with them—in other words, when patients had *agency* in the situation.

So far, so good. We've looked at firms and organizations doing meaningful things in terms of equity of consumption and delivering more by way of marketplace dignity to their customers in the real world and in tangible ways.

Of course, physical space can also be shaped in ways that deny dignity and perpetuate inequality. US history is, sadly, riddled with physical segregation in housing, education, healthcare, transportation, and more along racial lines. But the United States is not unique. Some of the worst offenders currently are among some of the other advanced economies in the world.

London is one of the world's megacities: vibrant and boasting extraordinary architecture, art, commerce, and culture; where communities from around the world and households of very diverse means and socioeconomic backgrounds live effectively cheek by jowl. But however egalitarian that might sound on paper, the reality is that today, the UK capital is also home to some astonishing realty and housing practices: practices that are positively Dickensian in the way that they seek to segregate the population into those who have and those who have not.

"Poor doors" are housing developments in London that feature separate blocks, entrances, and amenities for residents of local government-subsidized, socialized housing. They are a feature of the landscape in the majority of the city's neighborhoods and boroughs, and they are wildly unpopular. Despite being decried by many as "social apartheid" and numerous attempts to have the practice abolished, London's poor doors persist.[33]

Not to be outdone by their UK counterparts, American cities have also seen segregated building entrances for residents with lower means. In New York, for instance, households who were beneficiaries of affordable housing incentives not only saw themselves obliged to enter their homes using "poor doors" but also often had access to completely different amenities and facilities. In response to outrage created by the development company Extell's plans to use such a design in their new luxury housing development, Mayor Bill de Blasio banned New York's poor doors in 2015. But that just led developers to instead create completely separate "poor buildings."[34]

Equitable housing advocates on both sides of the Atlantic continue to anxiously scrutinize practices like these, seeing them as an affront to human dignity and a major concern for sustainable growth. For developers and city authorities, the race for profit may well continue to fuel things like poor doors, but what does the longer-term impact look like, especially in markets where historic volatility and the quest for profits at any cost have destabilized entire economies? We would argue that any step to prioritize the equality of customer dignity will have a stabilizing effect over time, forge better corporate reputations, and inevitably help to calm the waters of social discontent—good news for countries like the United Kingdom and the United States, in particular, riven by the polarization of wealth, opportunity, and political allegiance.

Housing is a major consideration. But there are many other contexts in which physical space can afford organizations the opportunity to affirm or compromise consumption equity for their customers.

Similarly, implementing rewards or costs related to consumption can be dignity-denying or -affirming. In a study when participants learned about a company that introduced either a health premium surcharge for its employees who were overweight or a discount for employees who were at a healthy weight, even though the financial consequences of the two policies were equivalent, people inferred different meanings. People inferred that the company held negative attitudes toward employees who were overweight only when they were told of the surcharge (i.e., a penalty). Specifically, people with higher body mass indexes reported that they would feel more stigmatized at work and would look for employment elsewhere if their employer offered an overweight surcharge than if it offered a healthy weight reward.[35]

We should note that consumers do recognize that differences in the service provided to various segments can be part of a justifiable service model. For example, airline passengers understand that those who fly millions of miles may receive perks that the occasional passenger will not. However, this, in itself, does not deny the dignity of the casual traveler. What *will* undermine dignity, however, would be the application of different rules for consumption to different groups. If, for example, travelers from one continent needed to earn only 10,000 miles to reach a certain status and enjoy the consumption benefits that accompany that status, while others needed to earn 20,000 miles, the dignity of the latter group would be denied. Fairness in consumption is critical—as is its communication.

To assess whether to offer a fair and equitable experience to all customers who have purchased your products or services, ask yourself these three key questions:

- Have you used technology to equalize people's ability to take advantage of the full range of consumption opportunities your product offers?
- Does the physical or virtual space in which people consume your product reinforce equity or suggest hierarchy?
- Do consumers know that any incentives or costs created during consumption are fairly administered, equally accessible to all, and consistent in their implementation?

What do your answers reveal to you about the experience your customers have as they actively consume your brand? Are there areas that you can improve upon, and if so, what kinds of steps can you to take to action this?

When you convert a potential client into a paying customer, you have achieved a clear business goal. But an even better outcome for your long-term strategy is to deliver an experience that makes your customer feel represented, that their agency and their interaction with you feel fair and equitable.

A customer whose marketplace dignity is affirmed by the consumption experience that you offer is a customer who is more likely to come back to you for future purchases. This is a customer who is more likely to spend more on your goods and services, to respond more favorably to your marketing efforts and advertisements, and to share the word about your brand with other potential customers. Building the loyalty of your customers is a big win for you and your organization, as we shall explore in chapter 5.

Chapter 4: Key Insights and Takeaways

- Dignity matters to your customers at the consumption phase—when they make the purchase and experience your products.
- Use the three levers of our Marketplace Dignity Framework to ensure that you get dignity right in your customers' experience with you: representation, agency, and equality.
- Representation: Find ways to build all your customers' needs into their experience of your services and products, and remember to respect their privacy.
- Agency: Remind your customers that they are in control, and where their choices and options are limited by circumstance, find ways to solicit their permission and opinions.
- Equality: Try to ensure that the experience you offer is the same for all your customers and that any incentives or costs are fairly administered. Seek feedback to ensure that you are not sending inadvertent messages of inequality in how you are framing your experience.

Chapter 5

Marketplace Dignity at the Post-Consumption Phase
Making It Stick Without Making It Hurt

I f we asked you to name a soda, what would you say? Chances are
that many of you would respond: Coca-Cola (or maybe just Coke).
And there's a good reason for this. For more than 100 years, the Coca-
Cola company has been slaking thirst all over the world. From its
humble origins as a flavored syrup sold in Atlanta pharmacies, it has
grown to be a $43 billion multinational behemoth,[1] selling to cus-
tomers in more than 200 countries worldwide. The "real thing" is one
of the planet's best-known and most loved brands. According to
Coke, 94% of the world's population recognizes its iconic red-and-
white logo.[2]

Brand recognition is one thing, but what about Coke's active customer base? Let's take a look at some stats.

Coca-Cola has a global social media fan base, boasting just short
of 110 million followers on Facebook alone. Posts are shared in a
plethora of languages. They feature campaigns, advertisements, special offers (including a well-known international campaign that
enabled customers to order the soda with their own name on the
bottle or can), sponsored events, and more—all of them built around
the concept of inclusion, diversity, community, and sharing.

"Share a Coke" is one of the company's most successful marketing gambits. Launched in Australia in 2011, the campaign saw Coca-
Cola reach almost 50% of the population by branding its packaging
with 150 popular names. In total, they sold more than 250 million

servings to a population of fewer than 23 million people. That is a lot of repeat business. The campaign was so well received that it expanded out across seventy more countries and 17,000 names. As Tasneem Kibria wrote in the *Business Standard*, "Rather than focusing on the product itself, the company focuses on an abstract positive concept—a connection between happiness and wellness. Every year, Coca-Cola has played a part in happy occasions around the globe—Ramadan, Eid, Christmas, festivals, or even seasonal branding—coke adverts show that coke brings people together, it helps to start conversations and spread the joy through giving Coca-Cola. . . . Besides, it targeted the most personal thing humans possess—our names—and this concept made 'sharing a coke' possible as it was more about giving the coke to someone."[3]

And the result of all this community building? Look at the numbers.

- Among the 96% of US respondents who know Coca-Cola, 64% of people use the brand.
- Around 52% of soft drink drinkers in the US say they are likely to use Coca-Cola again.
- In relation to the 61% usage share of the brand, this means that 85% of their drinkers show loyalty to the brand.[4]

How has Coca-Cola managed to garner so much customer loyalty? Here's what the company's North America CMO, Melanie Boulden, had to say: "It's about building trust, not buying trust. Earlier in my career, I might have said you gain trust with consumers by spending lots of dollars on advertising. How often you say something is important, but it's also what you're saying—and when and where you're saying it—that determine whether consumers really hear the message. We gain trust through authentic conversations, actions, and experiences when we provide information in a very transparent and connected way."[5]

The easiest sale, they say, is a repeat sale. Having persuaded someone to buy from you once, you have every chance that they will buy from you again. It is one of the great adages of business: acquiring new customers costs five times more than retaining them.[6]

Studies and reports reveal the following:

- 52% of customers would make an effort to buy from their favorite brand.
- There is a 60% to 70% chance of selling to an existing customer.
- 80% of profits come from 20% of loyal customers.
- Current customers are 50% more likely to purchase new products, and 31% are more likely to spend more on their purchases.
- Loyal customers are worth ten times more than the value of their first purchase.
- The spending of a loyal customer increases by 67% in their 31st to 36th months of doing business with a brand.[7]

No wonder the retained customer has become something of a holy grail for businesses worldwide.

Some, like Coca-Cola, seek to boost customer loyalty through campaigns like "Share a Coke," a campaign predicated on listening to customers and offering them genuine value. And in doing so, these brands also win themselves something of a seat at the table and a voice on some of the big societal issues, such as identity and community.

Others, less so. One of the biggest business trends in recent years has been subscription businesses, which have seen revenues grow by more than 430% in the last decade. The problem with many of these businesses is that they do not let their customers unsubscribe very easily. Certain areas of the press, media, and energy giants have a bad reputation in this sense, deploying tactics like auto-renewal or deliberately difficult unsubscribe processes to keep clients locked into repeat payments.[8]

Some create gardens of interconnected services with walls so high that it's always too painful to leave. Others find ways to hide the opt-out options. And having effected that change, plenty of firms find that they can raise rates at will, switch up the contract at their convenience, and load up loyalty benefits with so many arcane bureaucratic hassles that they'll never deliver what they promise. After all, if customers can't switch away from you, then you've essentially got a legal monopoly for yourself, at least among that group. It's a set of practices that gets catchily named "roach moteling," after the Roach Motel, the US brand of insect traps. Treating your customers as roaches won't set you up for success for very long.

First, an ethical approach is more likely to survive in a fast-evolving regulatory environment. In 2023, the US Federal Trade Commission proposed a new regulation called the "click to cancel" provision, requiring companies that offer subscription services online to make canceling them as easy as it was to sign up in the first place— just one of many proposed changes to the Negative Option rule, a measure enacted by the agency in 1973 that aimed to tamp down on predatory business practices.[9]

Then there's customer behavior itself. Remember that the benefits of customers' loyalty are not limited to repeat purchases; it also includes their willingness to buy new products and to recommend you to others. A resentfully trapped buyer certainly will not do that. Whatever loyalty to you such customers seem to have in a dashboard's churn statistics is in fact wholly spurious. Design your service and product in the right way—in ways that affirm the marketplace dignity of your customers once they've purchased from you—and you can build *genuine* loyalty that has a chance of lasting.

Let's look at this through the lens of our Marketplace Dignity Framework. And along the way, we'll showcase some examples of firms around the world that are doing this right, as well as a few of the many who are very far from doing so.

In the sections to come, we have dipped into experiences predominantly in emerging markets, where Tom's work on dignity is primarily focused and where interesting lessons for corporations globally can be readily learned.

Representation at the Post-Consumption Phase

Tom recently moved to Kenya and registered for a new bank account. He wanted to get the premium account, with a slightly higher fee. The staff immediately whisked him to a comfortable seat to talk to a personable salesperson. In a few minutes, the process was underway, and if he had any questions, he had the salesperson's business card. It was a seamless, thoughtful, swift consumer interaction.

Later that week, Tom had a question. It was answered immediately. The following week, there was some bureaucratic snafu that required him to come into the branch. Again, he was immediately shown to the same salesperson, who remembered his case and helped him address the problem.

Another week passed, and the account was up and running, and Tom's bank card had been delivered. The issue arose of how to register for online banking. Suddenly the salesperson who had previously been so helpful stopped replying to emails. Every online walkthrough pointed him back to the online banking portal, which wasn't working. This entailed another trip to the bank to meet face-to-face with a teller. When he got to the front of the line, Tom was met by a professional who was prompt, clear, and sympathetic. The problem was solved in a few minutes. Tom returned home and successfully logged in to the online banking system.

Standard Chartered Bank in Kenya overall performed pretty well when it came to representation. It was easy to get to a human—far easier than it is for many banks in richer countries. Tom felt seen and valued. The hitches arose each time the bank tried to communicate with him digitally.

In Kenya, of course, where the gross domestic product (GDP) per capita is around $2,000, staff salaries are comparatively cheap, and customers who can afford to pay a monthly fee for online banking are hard to come by. The calculations shake out differently in different economies. Still, the value of feeling seen, and of having human interactions, felt very great in Tom's experience. What can firms do to approach that experience when a human face feels like an expensive option? Clear updates on effort and progress make a difference.

Examining banking in the developing market of Uganda, the researchers Mabel Komunda (Makerere University) and Aihie Osarenkhoe (University of Gävle) have shown that when things go wrong, people care about how people communicate with them. Of course, the first thing that people want is for the problem to be resolved. Yet this research showed that even independent of this—regardless of whether the issue was resolved—how the bank communicated with its customers had a very significant and strongly positive relationship with their satisfaction. They were then more likely to say they would recommend the service to others.[10]

Similar results have been observed in a study of call centers in the Netherlands, which showed that customers simply cared whether they felt the representative had been attentive, regardless of whether they had been particularly perceptive or responsive. Attentiveness increased their satisfaction with the encounter in its own right.[11]

We spoke to Rafe Mazer, a longtime observer of business culture in emerging markets and then the director of the Consumer Protection Initiative at Innovations for Poverty Action (IPA).[12] He warned that consumers can quickly become "fatalistic" about poor post-consumption service. And with good reason: there are plenty of instances of abusive fee-charging practices, he says. Yet when the culture of an organization—a culture set, shaped, and modeled by its leadership—genuinely seeks to see and hear the needs and concerns of its customers and act on those insights, there is actually plenty that the organization can do. From the careful formatting of terms and conditions, to structures of repayment, to how firms share information with regulators, Mazer believes that organizations have tremendous agency in making their customers feel represented during and after consumption of their services.

He cites examples of businesses doing this well. One is Jumo, a UK-based fintech firm that supports access to digital financial services for people in emerging markets. Jumo routinely tests the user-friendliness of the terms and conditions that they offer on their loans and looks for any inherent bias in their credit-scoring algorithms. One test surfaced systemic problems with female customers in Zambia, a demographic that is historically a good credit risk but who do not have much available data about them. A "few tweaks," says Mazer, and Jumo was able to adjust for greater representation and inclusion—something he describes as "good for them, good for responsible, paying customers[,] and good for the industry in general."[13]

A multinational doing well in terms of hearing its customers is American Express, which ranked highest in customer satisfaction among credit card users for the fourth consecutive year in 2023, in the J. D. Power survey.[14] They have been lauded, among other things, for offering a 24/7 help line with secure messaging and an online chat—a massive boon to customers who need to address issues at work or outside office hours.

Perhaps one of the most important takeaways from Mazer's work is the need to "recognize the dignity costs of automation."[15] He (and we) would argue that to ensure that your customers still feel seen and heard once they have done business with you, you should always retain some sort of access to a human employee—even as you offer customers the option to not be contacted.

In 2016, Accenture's Global Consumer Pulse Research surveyed more than 24,000 customers in thirty-three countries and eleven industries around customer service. Eighty-three percent of US customers said they preferred dealing with human beings over digital channels, and 52% had switched providers in the past year due to poor service at an estimated cost of $1.6 trillion.

"Companies have lost sight of the importance of human interaction and often make it too difficult for consumers to get the right level of help and service that they need," said Robert Wollan, senior managing director, Advanced Customer Strategy, Accenture Strategy. "Companies wrongly assume that their digital-only customers are their most profitable, and that customer service is a cost."[16]

Whatever your organization, sector, geography, or client base looks like, ensuring that customers feel represented—being proactive about ways that they feel seen and heard—is a critical first step in their continuing journey with you beyond that initial purchase. To ensure that you are building loyalty through a lens of marketplace dignity, ask yourself these questions:

- What mechanisms or processes do you enact in your organization to listen to your existing customers and capture their ongoing needs or objectives?
- How do you use customer intelligence to shape their continuing journey with you? And what safeguards do you implement to protect your customers' privacy?
- In an age of increasing automation, how does your organization prioritize communicating with customers post-purchase? From your customers' perspective, would you say it was easy or difficult to engage with your brand on a human level?

Agency at the Post-Consumption Phase

The very moment that Tom opened an account with Standard Chartered Bank in Kenya, his phone began to buzz. A slew of unsolicited promotional messages started rolling in: refer a friend; transact at preferential foreign exchange rates; invest in global equities. On and on it went, until Tom eventually implemented a general spam block by his mobile provider, Safaricom, to stop the noise.

Tom briefly considered tweeting about his frustration. But that seemed like a last resort. Harried social media teams, poorly trained for the job, are often a de facto consumer complaints team without the resources to solve real problems. He preferred to go through the more typical channels first.

Frequently, the best chance of reaching a human is to call a service center. Yet this can be frustrating and can compromise marketplace dignity. The hours that customers lose in phone-menu loops, unable to select the right option or articulate a specific issue, are hours they'll never get back.

The well-known tech entrepreneur and former *Engadget* editor Ryan Block recorded and published an eight-minute interaction with Comcast customer care when he attempted to cancel his cable television service in 2014. Among the responses he received to his clear request to unsubscribe were:

- "Being that we are the number one provider of internet and TV service in the entire country, why do you not want to have the number one rated internet service available?"
- "So you're not interested in the fastest internet in the country?"
- "You don't want something that works? So why don't you want something that's good service and something that works?"
- "I'm really ashamed to see you go to something that can't give you what we can."
- "I could save you $100 . . . actually more than $100 per month!"

The recording went viral. *Time* ran the story with the headline: "Recording of Man's Attempt to Cancel Comcast Will Drive You Insane."[17]

Comcast was quick off the mark to try to claw back its good reputation, issuing a statement that described the interaction as "not consistent with how we train our customer service representatives." But social media users were equally quick to call Comcast out for being disingenuous. Call center workers were trained to be precisely like this, said one, adding, "These guys fight tooth and nail to keep every customer because if they don't meet their numbers they don't get paid. . . . Comcast literally provides an incentive for this kind of behavior. It's the same reason people's bills are always fucked up: people stuffing them with things they don't need or in some cases don't even agree to."[18]

What the Comcast imbroglio shows is that agency—the freedom of choice and action—should extend not only to the customer who has purchased from you, but perhaps also to the post-sale employees who manage queries, complaints, requests for help, and requests to cancel any subscription that a customer may have with you. Earlier in this chapter, we talked about a potential need for human interaction to affirm dignity in the purchase phase of your customer's journey. But the human touch will work only if your employees are given the agency to act like humans, not overtrained automatons.

There is another way. In a *Harvard Business Review* article, Tony Hsieh, CEO of the online shoe retailer Zappos (now owned by Amazon), recalls the lengths to which the firm went to create a good impression for customers:

> A lot of people may think it's strange that an internet company would be so focused on the telephone, when only about 5% of our sales happen by phone. But we've found that on average, our customers telephone us at least once at some point, and if we handle the call well, we have an opportunity to create an emotional impact and a lasting memory. We receive thousands of phone calls and emails every day, and we view each one as an opportunity to build the Zappos brand into being about the very best customer service. Our philosophy has been that most of the money we might ordinarily have spent on advertising should be invested in customer service, so that our customers will do the marketing for us through word of mouth.[19]

There are many steps that you can take to ensure that your customers experience agency in their ongoing relationship with you. Start by asking yourself these three questions:

- Do you share clear and simple options to stop receiving marketing communications or to pause or cancel subscriptions to your services or products?
- Are you transparent in your terms and conditions, such that your customers feel informed and empowered in their ability

to choose which service or pricing structure works best for them?

- Do you prioritize retaining customers at any cost? Is the fear of losing customers so great that you make it hard for them to leave you? Or do you believe in their agency to leave and come back to you at a future date?

Equality at the Post-Consumption Phase

When things go wrong in a consumer relationship, any power differential between consumer and business that exists is fully exposed. For instance, Tom's mobile provider, Safaricom, is the largest telco in Kenya and one of the most profitable companies in East Africa. Its journey has been remarkable. The firm's incredibly rapid growth has made it absolutely central to the story of widespread phone access in Kenya. Safaricom dominates the telco industry in Kenya with a subscriber base of almost 47 million in 2023, in a country of 53 million. Their closest competitor, Airtel, had around 18 million members.[20]

The firm has consistently offered amazing innovations that have really helped the agency of customers: the popular Please Call Me function allows customers with no money to pay for airtime to invite friends to call them instead. Its M-Shwari and Fuliza loan products have provided access to capital. Best in class, though, is probably its M-PESA service, which since 2007 has powered incredibly easy money transfers for almost all its customers—a service that puts it far ahead of payment providers anywhere in the world and which products like Apple Pay are only just beginning to match in richer countries. Even tiny, informal businesses have been able to easily manage their money at a time when banks would never serve them. Research has shown that the first few years of access to M-PESA alone pulled almost 200,000 households out of poverty and significantly increased per-capita consumption across the country.[21]

Safaricom has enjoyed vast popularity in Kenya. When its former CEO, Bob Collymore, died in 2019, there was widespread popular sadness and generous tributes from politicians and journalists. However, M-PESA's incredible success has also seen Safaricom become a functional monopoly in Kenya. Complaints about prices for M-PESA transactions and for airtime and data have begun to mount. All users receive several marketing text messages a day, as well as flash Short Message Services that take over the phone screen, regardless of whether one actively accesses it.

The frustration came to a head in 2022, when the government issued a requirement that all telcos update their user details or have their mobile line closed down and face a fine of 300,000 Kenyan shillings (at the time, approximately $2,500) and up. Ostensibly the measure is to combat corruption and fight terrorism, but details on how this will help are vague. While other telecom providers have allowed people to complete their reregistration online, Safaricom high-handedly insisted that all customers come in person to its shops. Safaricom leadership and government figures (the government is a 35% shareholder) have given conflicting messages on what information is required. After critics pointed out that they registered their details when they originally got their subscriber identity module (SIM) cards, it was rebranded as a "verification" exercise.

There are worries that the exercise undermines privacy, that the data may be exploited by government figures seeking reelection, and that this is no way to treat customers with better things to do with their day. One customer, Mercy Makau, spoke to the Kenyan newspaper *The Star*, saying: "Last week, I checked my registration details and I received a message clearly stating that my SIM card was fully registered. On Tuesday, I decided to just check again since some people were giving different accounts. This time around, the message I received stated that my sim [sic] card registration is now incomplete."[22]

Another user asked Safaricom via Twitter what would happen to her outstanding M-Shwari loan if she did not reregister. The company said that she would be reported to the Credit Reference Bureau (presumably using details that they already had at hand, and obviating the need for any further details to be registered).[23]

This is now a form of dignity denial by a company that had previously worked hard to affirm marketplace dignity. People continue to be loyal, but only because they have no choice; an effective regulator would have separated M-PESA from Safaricom long ago and ensured that customers could choose from a range of mobile networks without losing access to the financial services that everyone needs. In 2018, the Central Bank of Kenya made such an order, but only in 2022 did Safaricom partially comply. This gave Airtel and Telkom interoperable access to one part of the M-PESA service—direct payments between lines. However, payment of bills, another popular service, had to wait another year while the firm waited "to gauge the success of till number access by other telcos."[24] As of November 2023, it still has not been instituted in full.

Powerful firms can choose to act in this way. They can ignore customer complaints and defend themselves with more legal firepower than any individual can muster. But at what cost in the long term?

Safaricom was ranked by *Forbes* as Africa's best employer, 67th in the world, in 2018. By 2023, it had dropped to 164th place.[25] Fed-up customers began seeking to redress the power imbalance through lawsuits. A class action suit to the value of $2.38 billion was brought by M-PESA users who accused the company of profit-making financial lending without consent and in violation of Kenya's Banking Act.[26]

Safaricom's woes are by no means unique. But they do exemplify the risks inherent in exploiting power differentials between organizations and customers who have reached an impasse in the postpurchase phase.

Other firms have found that a better approach is humility. Organizations like Apple, KFC, Netflix, and Airbnb have won plaudits from customers (as well as the media) for sincere, authentic, and human apologies—typically issued directly by the CEO—when things go wrong in their relationship with engaged consumers. For instance, when Airbnb was accused of racial profiling and discrimination against Black customers in 2015, it found itself in a social media storm and facing possible class action lawsuits. The CEO, Brian Chesky, immediately issued a statement that read: "Bias and discrimination have no place on Airbnb, and we have zero tolerance for them. Unfortunately, we have been slow to address these problems, and for this I am sorry. I take responsibility for any pain or frustration this has caused members of our community. We will not only make this right; we will work to set an example that other companies can follow."[27]

Affirming the equality of all your customers—both in relation to each other and in relation to your organization—underscores their marketplace dignity and helps drive the loyalty that they feel toward you and your brand. Airbnb is just one organization that has sought to do this and that has seen customers return and business boom—this despite the pandemic hitting their revenue and workforce like a hammer in 2020. By 2023, the firm was back to posting record revenue and profits.[28]

Does your organization do its best to support the equitable treatment of all your customers in their continuing journey with your services and products? Ask yourself these three questions:

- When things go wrong, do you react like humans, or do you have a tendency to retreat into your corporate power to avoid consequences?
- Are you prepared to take responsibility and apologize to our customers openly, sincerely, and transparently? If so, who takes on this role within the organization?
- What do you do as an organization to capture the learning that accompanies problems in your customer care and service? How do you ensure that you can and will do better by your customers going forward?

We have now walked through the major steps in your customer journey; from pre-consumption to evaluation, from consumption to the post-consumption phase. To help you map this journey and design for marketplace dignity, we have shared a framework with you that pulls the levers of representation, agency, and equality. These are levers that you can use to ensure that your customers feel seen and heard, empowered, and treated with equal respect at every touch point of their experience with you and your brand. And we have asked you some questions—many of them difficult to answer.

We urge you to think about each of the questions that we've put to you in this chapter and the chapters that precede it. Doing so will help you do the following:

- Systematically analyze your firm's processes and practices through a new lens of marketplace dignity.
- Assess where you are right now as an organization and pinpoint areas for improvement.
- Make a systemic shift in your thinking about marketplace dignity as something that is not just nice to do, but critical to the long-term success of your business.

If you have read this far, you have already come a long way toward rethinking your relationship with your customers. You have understood that long-term *profit* and authentic *purpose* are essentially undergirded by *people*—and that people have an *inherent and innate right to human dignity*. Affirm this; and you have seen by now some of the many benefits that will accrue to your business, your culture, your processes and practices, and your longevity. Deny marketplace dignity—intentionally or accidentally—and you have understood some of the risks that lie ahead.

We believe that there is a clear and inalienable business case for intentionally and purposefully acting to affirm marketplace dignity at every phase of your customer journey. We believe that marketplace dignity will unlock new sources of value for you and your organization. And perhaps most important, we believe that marketplace dignity—treating your customers in a way that respects them as human beings—is quite simply the right thing to do.

To help you integrate marketplace dignity into every touch point of your customer journey, we have shared with you our Marketplace

Dignity Framework—a framework predicated on the three levers of human dignity: representation, agency, and equality. Our framework sets out how and why these three levers intersect with each phase of your customer journey, and it posits clear questions that you should ask to ensure that you are doing your best to respect their dignity in meaningful ways. We have also shared with you some examples from the field, from a diversity of organizations and sectors and from all around the world, to help flesh out these ideas and questions in a practical sense.

In chapter 6, we would like you to consider a real-life business case yourself and see if, using the Marketplace Dignity Framework, you can make sense of what happened. Looking at your customer journey through the lens of marketplace dignity is another powerful tool that will help you diagnose missteps and correct them; and conversely, unpack why things work when they do, and better employ best practices. We shall see this in the next discussion.

Chapter 5: Key Insights and Takeaways

- Dignity matters to your customers at the phase when they interact with you (e.g., when they want to modify their purchase or need help). Building a loyal customer base brings more benefits to your organization over and above securing the immediate sale. Affirming marketplace dignity is fundamentally important if you want your customers to come back, to buy more from you, and to recommend your organization to others.
- Again, our Marketplace Dignity Framework can help you to build the loyalty of your customers through representation, agency, and equality.
- Representation: Ensure that you have the resources in place, including the human touch, to capture your customers' feedback such that they feel seen and heard.
- Agency: Let your customers go if they want to leave. Don't make it difficult for them; instead, trust that your goods and

services have the dignity-affirming quality and appeal to win them back.

- Equality: Apologize to your customers when things go wrong, and thank them when they go right. Be human in all your interactions with all your customers, and make sure to put the mechanisms in place to capture anything that you learn from them.

Chapter 6

Marketplace Dignity
A New Conversation Begins

I n this book, we have shared our Marketplace Dignity Framework with you, and we've seen how this framework plays out across the customer journey. Along the way, we've looked at examples of firms who have done things well or not so well at different touch points in that journey.

Now we'd like to put you in the driver's seat. We would like to invite you to look at another real-world scenario to see if you can pinpoint some complex dynamics at play through the lens of dignity. Consider the following case.

A few years ago, Cait received an invitation to consult with a pioneering healthcare company. The firm in question had developed a long-acting, injectable medication to treat a very serious mental illness. It would deliver months of medication in each dose. Bringing this medication to market and rolling it out effectively had the potential to transform the lives of patients and their caregivers. Now, one of the major challenges in treating this illness has historically been patients' inability or unwillingness to stick to a stringent medication schedule. By choice or accident, these patients would often miss a pill here or there, and when they did, their lives could unravel in very visible and devastating ways. Cait's client had come up with something stunning: a simple injection that could treat this condition while minimizing the risks of ill effects such as psychiatric hospitalization or suicidal ideation often associated with the reluctance or avoidance of oral medication.[1] And they had gotten off to a promising start.

It was abundantly clear that everyone on the medication team, from clinical researchers to biostatisticians to lab technicians, cared very deeply about the people that they hoped to serve. Talking to the team, Cait was struck by how assiduously the firm had kept patients at the very center of the development process. They had gone the extra mile in surveying patients, clinicians, and caregivers to ensure that they heard and understood needs, pain points, and the concomitant dosage and timing options that made the most sense. And their marketing efforts were no less meticulous. Every advertisement or brochure they sent out strove to fully represent people suffering from this illness as valid and to value them as the human beings that this firm knew them to be.

What's more, the team was confident that their solution would empower patients to care for themselves in the long term. They envisioned a future where people would have the agency to manage their own medication for months after the first injection rather than having to rely on others to remember their daily pill—or help them manage the fallout of a missed dose. This really mattered to the firm, and they went about investing time and creativity in setting up systems to help patients maintain that kind of ongoing autonomy.

From the outside, this was a company that was absolutely committed to human dignity. Theirs was a product expressly designed to prioritize the dignity of patients whose dignity had been compromised by mental illness. And in the development of that product, they had gone to some trouble to give voice to their customers and include them in their design processes. All their efforts were focused on empowering people suffering with a debilitating and often stigmatized condition, and treating them as equals. Everything was in place to change people's lives for the better.

But then something stalled. Instead of welcoming this new drug, patients coming into the examining room balked at the idea of having the injection. No matter how enthusiastically doctors extolled the advantages of the treatment, these patients refused. Sitting there, with the option of something as simple as a quick jab that would deliver months of medication—a solution brilliantly designed to obviate all the risks of missing their daily pill—these people still said no. It wasn't empowering, they said. Quite the opposite. Being offered this new treatment made them feel harassed and actually dehumanized. Patients walked out of the consulting room in droves, and the injectable drug went no further. Months of dedicated work amounted to nothing.

We'd like you to stop now for a moment.

Based on everything that you have read in the previous chapters of this book, ask yourself: What do you think went wrong here? At which point in the customer journey did everything unravel for Cait's client? Were these customers inadequately represented? Was their agency compromised? Or were they treated as somehow less than equal?

Remember that this is a company that had taken great pains to assert the dignity of their customers in the design and marketing of their new product. Their goal was to improve people's quality of life. They had focused efforts on solving a major need, and if successful, their product would empower these people with the wherewithal to manage their condition over the longer term. As far as the company was concerned, they had affirmed the representation, agency, and equality of their patients—wasn't that their very purpose in developing this new drug in the first place? So much of what they did was right that they were totally dumbfounded when things suddenly went wrong.

Now let's look at Cait's story again using the Marketplace Dignity Framework.

Developing the drug had worked well for dignity in the preconsumption phase. The product met real-world needs and addressed the right pain points. Bringing it to market, medical professionals and caregivers had been convinced of its efficacy and benefits. The post-consumption outlook appeared to affirm dignity. But at the point of *evaluation*—at the moment of decision-making—patients chose not to consume the product. Of course, some said that they were afraid of needles. But that wasn't the main objection. The overwhelming majority claimed that being offered a one-off injection there in their doctor's office denied them their dignity.

Yes, taking a pill every day came with its problems, they told doctors. But at least *they could choose* to take the pill or not. Living with a chronic mental illness meant living in a world where your agency and control over your own life are severely and constantly constricted. For these people, the choices that others enjoy are not the same: say, the freedom to drive a car, to travel, to change jobs or career, or to make new friends—they have very little agency over things that others take for granted. And the one thing they felt any agency about? Taking that pill.

What this company had failed to understand was the importance of asserting marketplace dignity at the *point of evaluation*. Specifically, they had failed to fully affirm their *customers' agency* at this critical moment in their journey. There, in the examining room, these customers were being asked to roll up their sleeves and passively accept an injection. Doing so could minimize a bunch of risks further down the line, for sure. But it also meant handing absolute control to a clinician at that critical moment. And it meant relinquishing their customary, daily control of their own medication for many weeks or months to come.

Looking at this through a dignity lens, it now became clear to Cait's client why these patients were reluctant to consume. They had underestimated the need for agency in evaluation. As it turned out, this was the one touch point where they hadn't watched and listened. Rather, they had done their research far outside that key decision-making context, where people gave the more "rational" response. To understand the moment of choice, they would have had to partner with people outside their company—with doctors, nurses, and other caregivers—to better grasp the dynamics at work in situ and in real life. Of course, they would have to do it in a way that respected true representation—people's need to be seen or not seen.

The good news is that over time, other companies have been successful in rolling out these kinds of injectable drugs. As a primary treatment for chronic mental illness, they are gaining serious traction and delivering dignity-affirming benefits. Patients report that they feel these drugs do a good job representing them, in the sense that they can be seen as themselves: they feel more normal, less abnormal; more equal; and more empowered as a result.

The bad news for Cait's client is that these are opportunities that they missed out on, despite their excellent intentions and painstaking efforts to do the right thing by their patients. Had they thought about marketplace dignity at each specific touch point in the customer journey, they might have been better prepared when things came to a head in the examining room.

There's something important that we need to say at this point: No one gets marketplace dignity right or wrong all the time. No company does a consistently good or poor job of respecting the dignity of their customers. We all make mistakes, and we all get things right. *Nobody gets dignity all right or all wrong all the time.*

The examples that we have shared throughout this book—including the example that we have just shared with you in this chapter—all come from companies that have done great things by their customers despite the occasional mishap; others champion marketplace dignity at specific points in their customer journey, but they are just as prone to making mistakes as any other organization at different touch points.

We have seen how Sephora, Walmart, and Universal Standard have at times designed well for representation, agency, and equality at the evaluation phase, for instance. Similarly, we have looked at how Peloton seemed to drop the ball on representation in the preconsumption phase, and yet delivered a consumption experience that was so dignity-affirming across all three parameters of our framework that they have built an extensive and loyal customer base. Elsewhere, we have talked about failures in representation, agency, and equality that have sometimes created bad press for PepsiCo,

Burger King, and Apple—organizations that at other times have nailed marketplace dignity.

Every organization and firm that we have worked with, researched, or interacted with as customers does some things right and other things wrong. Being consistent about marketplace dignity is inherently hard. Whatever your organization or sector, there are typically so many different agents that interact with your customers at different touch points in their journey that it feels impossible to design for dignity everywhere and at all times. So what can you do?

Think again about Cait's client. Working with Cait to view the customer journey through the lens of marketplace dignity, this company was able to pinpoint exactly where they went wrong and why. They could see and understand what had happened. And going forward, they could use this knowledge to design better to recognize the dignity of their customers. They learned. And in learning, they were empowered.

Understanding the importance of marketplace dignity, and how it is affirmed or denied and the touch points in your customer journey, will empower you and your organization. If you can see where you might have dropped the ball—if you can understand how a problem happened and why it mattered to your customers—you are in a better position to take stock, correct, repair, and readjust. You have much greater clarity on where other missteps might occur and take steps to redesign your customer journey to prevent them from happening, or at the very least respond quickly and effectively when they do.

In our work with clients, there are invariably "aha" moments that are hugely rewarding to them and to us: moments of realization when organizations pinpoint a denial of dignity—however unintentional—and grasp new opportunities to learn, adjust, and redesign. We love seeing this happen. For Cait's client, making sense of what happened with their drug was a chance to convert failure into growth—an understanding of their customer base predicated not only on medical needs, but on the human need for dignity. And for an organization so inherently focused on restoring, enhancing, and preserving human dignity, this was a stunning moment of discovery.

Of course, this kind of learning should not be limited to failures or mistakes. It is every bit as important to use the lens of market-place dignity to look at those things that you are doing well. There's so much to be gained in understanding why these things work and why they are important. For us, it's just as gratifying when a client uses our framework to analyze their successes. Instead of simply see-ing certain practices or processes as "socially sensitive" or "customer oriented," they can now appreciate how these things proactively affirm the dignity of their customers in different ways and at different touch points. Armed with this new understanding, they are better able to define, replicate, and employ best practices. They are in a stronger position to defend their choices, justify their budget, deploy resources, and optimize their customers' experiences.

So how does all this apply to you and your organization? In this book, we have shared with you a way of understanding why your cus-tomers behave the way they do. We have invited you to reconsider what makes them engage or disengage with you, your brand, and your products and services. We have looked at the rational and affec-tive systems that have dominated trade and commerce for time immemorial: reason being the cognitive, the more deliberate way that we process information and make choices based on data; and appe-tite, the intuitive or affective element that relates to the more impul-sive, emotional drivers of human decision-making. And we have asked you to consider a third dynamic, a third system, in a sense. We've asked you to think about dignity.

But we're not asking you to invent a new wheel to do this. We're also offering you a tool to use when thinking about the dignity of your customers. And we've shown you how that tool works at the different touch points in their journey, and how it is predicated on the three levers of representation, agency, and equality throughout.

Perhaps a good place for you to start is to stand back and take a look at your customer journey with your brand. Maybe begin by homing in on the things that you are already doing that create traction—things that do seem to drive awareness and consideration, that convert customers; things that you currently do that seem to build loyalty and retention. What are those things? And ask: *Why are they working*? Are you simply doing something "nice" (which, by the way, is a comment that we have heard from our corporate clients more than once)? Or are you doing things that make more sense viewed through a dignity lens? How are you affirming dignity right now? And you might now be better able to unpack and use these things in other ways, such that you can do the following:

- Unlock new value for your brand.
- Drive your reputation and brand consistency.
- Claim a seat at the table on the issues that matter.
- Do all of the above at minimal cost and with minimal outlay.

We don't have a hard-and-fast rule here for you. Every organization is unique; every organization is different. And so is every customer.

Your setting, your context, your pain points, and your strong suits are highly specific to you and your firm. And when you look at your business through the framework we have shared in this book, you will discover specific things. You may find that you are doing a great job with representation at the pre-consumption phase. Or maybe your strong suit is equality in post-consumption. Or it could be that customer agency in consumption is a challenge that you will want to address in some way. We believe that for you, the magic will happen when you apply the Marketplace Dignity Framework in your own business.

And by *you*, we mean whoever you are and whatever role you currently play within your organization. You may be the CEO of your business, or you may be working in marketing or human resources, research and development, or customer services. We believe that in an ideal world, every business would have a Tom Wein—a dedicated champion of marketplace dignity with the authority, the influence, and the resources to oversee your customer journey from start to finish and to design for human dignity at every inflection point. But we're realistic enough to know that we are not in an ideal world. We also know that marketplace dignity is in many ways something novel: a new way of looking at your market and making sense of your customer base.

Dignity is, of course, nothing new. From Plato writing about the human spirit almost 2,500 years ago to the United Nations Universal of Human Rights of 1948, human beings have pondered dignity for millennia—agreeing and disagreeing over what dignity means, how it manifests, and why it matters; whether dignity is something that can be understood in terms of behavior or identity. This is a conversation with tendrils that extend into every area of human endeavor and society. And conversations around dignity are not new.

What is perhaps new is *how we apply the concept of dignity to our customers* and how we work to affirm that dignity in every aspect of the experience that we offer them and every touch point of the engagement that we have with them. Marketplace dignity is perhaps, in this sense, a new idea. It is perhaps a new conversation—and a conversation that we would very much like to continue having with you.

It is our hope that this book will empower you to diagnose, understand, and enhance the way that you engage with your customer base across the entirety of their journey. And we urge you to get out there and put some of these ideas into action. We would also like you to share what you learn with us. Let us know what you find. Report back and share your discoveries, your doubts, your insights, and your own "aha" moments. You'll find our contact details in the epilogue of this book, and we look forward to hearing back from you. We want to have that conversation with you as we continue to learn together. And it is a conversation that we must have.

Marketplace dignity is as core an imperative as every other priority or exigency your business has. We believe it is as critical to your viability as are your strategy, your purpose, the values you espouse, and the processes and procedures that your organization enacts to preserve productivity and drive your bottom line. Understand this, and you have understood the marketplace dignity imperative. Understand this, and you are already on your way to making dignity a critical function of your customers' experience with you at every touch point, at every turn.

We wish you success, enlightenment, and greater discoveries on the journey ahead. It is our honor and our pleasure to join you on that journey.

Epilogue

Coming together as a trio to write this book has been a rich exchange of ideas and a profound reflection on the inalienable importance of human dignity from three distinct perspectives. Just as there is a *business case* for dignity, the three of us believe that there is an equally powerful and compelling *moral case* for doing the right thing. Human beings forge communities. A defining feature of human behavior is to assemble in groups and collaborate with each other for protection and productivity. We do this most successfully when there is an understanding that we're all in this together; when there's a *contract* between us that fundamentally respects our humanity and our dignity as collaborators, regardless of our individual contributions. We believe that businesses, as communities of human beings, are not exempt from this contract. We believe that businesses share a human imperative to do what's best for the community that they exist within, and to prioritize what is important for society as a whole. And this has been borne out in our collective experience working with organizations around the world.

Optimism has been in short supply recently, and the challenges ahead are vast. The last few years have been very hard for very many of us. We have had to grapple with grief, with a lost sense of self and with profound changes in the way we live and work. Collectively, we have come through a huge storm. And even as we rebuild, there are enormous risks and challenges ahead. But in our work, we are also seeing an *opening up*—opportunities for different conversations about how we live and collaborate. Part of what we are seeing is the emergence of purpose and values as rock-solid ideas, as well as the vocabulary of dignity and enabling—allowing us to have new conversations about how we move forward.

Marketplace dignity is a conversation that we welcome you to join and to drive. We look forward to learning *with* you and *from* you as you advance the marketplace dignity imperative in your role, in your function, and within your organization.

If you wish to contact us, you can do so at the email address marketplacedignity@gmail.com.

Cait, Neela, and Tom

Acknowledgments

We are grateful to the many people who encouraged us and with whom we have developed and debated these ideas—especially Sakshi Ghai, Heather Lanthorn, Torben Fischer, Paul Perrin, and Mallika Sobti.

Cait expresses her appreciation to the many seminar participants, students, colleagues, and fellow researchers who have both welcomed and challenged the idea of consumer dignity. Turning this from a vague idea to a practical set of tools was possible only because of their encouragement and insight. Further, she expresses her gratitude to the Wharton School, her students and colleagues, who have encouraged her to explore this topic—being around a group of people passionately committed to pushing the boundaries of traditionally defined "business" is a gift and an inspiration.

Neela expresses her gratitude to her husband, Tanuj, for being her biggest supporter, reading early versions of the book and providing practical suggestions; and to her daughter, Aliya, for continually asking when the book was being published. She has also immensely benefited from discussions with so many generous people. In addition to those already mentioned, she is also grateful to Heidi McAnnally-Linz, Matias Nestore, and Katie Stanford at The Life You Can Save; along with Michael Eddy, Freddy Bharucha, Nachiket Mor, Ruth Levine, Catherine Thomas, Indradeep Ghosh, Shaurya Salwan, Allison Yates-Berg, and Anthony Barrows.

Tom expresses his gratitude to IDinsight, and especially to their former CEO, Ruth Levine, whose support allowed the founding and funding of the Dignity Initiative. His colleagues on that team have been vital to this journey: Nakubyana Mungomba, Meltreen Sikele

Wanyonyi, Dilshad S., and Mary Blair. He is forever awed by the brilliance of his partner, Rachel Strohm.

Finally, we are grateful to the many thousands of research participants who have shared a little piece of their lives with us. Our work would be nothing without them.

Notes

Introduction

1 The United Nations, Universal Declaration of Human Rights, December 10, 1948, https://www.un.org/en/about-us/universal-declaration-of-human-rights.

2 Tom Wein, Sakshi Ghai, Cait Lamberton, and Neela A. Saldanha, "The Psychology of Consumer Dignity," in *The Cambridge Handbook of Consumer Psychology*, ed. Cait Lamberton, Derek D. Rucker, and Stephen A. Spiller (Cambridge University Press, 2023), 387–415.

3 Wein et al., "The Psychology of Consumer Dignity."

4 Wein et al.

Chapter 1

1 David Gianatasio, "Mountain Dew Makes the Best Ad Ever with a Violent Talking Goat," *Adweek,* March 20, 2013, https://www.adweek.com/creativity /mountain-dew-makes-best-ad-ever-violent-talking-goat-148055.

2 Eyder Peralta, "Mountain Dew Pulls Ad Called 'Most Racist . . . in History,'" NPR, May 1, 2013, https://www.npr.org/sections/thetwo-way/2013/05/01 /180379414/mountain-dew-pulls-ad-called-most-racist-in-history.

3 Seb Joseph, "PepsiCo Pulls Ad After Racist Claims," *Marketing Week*, May 2, 2013, https://www.marketingweek.com/pepsico-pulls-ad-after-racist-claims/.

4 Adam Gabbatt, "Coffee Shop Racism: Where America's Racial Divisions Are Exposed," *The Guardian*, May 28, 2018, https://www.theguardian.com/world /2018/may/28/coffee-shop-racism-starbucks-arrests.

5 Maggie Astor, "Dove Drops an Ad Accused of Racism," *New York Times*, October 8, 2017, https://www.nytimes.com/2017/10/08/business/dove-ad-racist .html.

6 Lucy Tesseras, "'Sneaky Sexism' Is on the Rise in Advertising," *Marketingweek*, March 8, 2021, https://www.marketingweek.com/sneaky-sexism-advertising/.

7 Avi Dan, "Dove Invented 'Femvertising' but Its Latest Stunt Didn't Wash with Consumers," *Forbes*, May 11, 2017, https://www.forbes.com/sites/avidan/2017/05 /11/dove-invented-femvertising-but-its-latest-stunt-didnt-wash-with-consumers /?sh=612cd09556b6.

8 Wein et al., "The Psychology of Consumer Dignity."

9   Accenture, "Accenture Life Trends 2023," 2023, *Accenture Report*, https://www
    .accenture.com/content/dam/accenture/final/capabilities/song/marketing
    -transformation/document/Accenture-Life-Trends-2023-Full-Report.pdf.

10 Cait Lamberton, Neela Saldanha, and Sakshi Ghai, "Introducing System Zero:
    The Drive for Marketplace Dignity," January 2020, https://papers.ssrn.com/sol3
    /papers.cfm?abstract_id=3745882.

11 Daniel Lubetzky, "You Can't Make Big ESG Commitments While Failing at the
    Basics of Kindness," *Fortune*, August 8, 2023, https://fortune.com/2023/08/08
    /daniel-lubetzky-big-esg-commitments-failng-basics-kindness-daniel-lubetzky/.

12 P. Fader, *Customer Centricity: Focus on the Right Customers for Strategic
    Advantage* (Wharton School Press, 2020).

13 Wein et al., "The Psychology of Consumer Dignity."

14 Dennis P. Carmody and Michael Lewis, "Brain Activation When Hearing One's
    Own and Others' Names," *Brain Research* 1116 (October 20, 2006): 153–58,
    https://www.ncbi.nlm.nih.gov/pmc/articles/PMC1647299/.

15 Tracy Rank-Christman, Maureen Morrin, and Chrisstine Ringler, "R-E-S-P-E-
    C-T, Find Out What My Name Means to Me: The Effects of Marketplace
    Misidentification on Consumption," *Journal of Consumer Psychology* 27, no. 3
    (July 2017): 333–40, https://doi.org/10.1016/j.jcps.2016.12.002.

16 Zainab Shafqat Adil, "Name Mispronunciations Leave Lasting Impact on
    Individuals," *The Standard*, June 10, 2021, https://standard.asl.org/18485
    /features/name-pronunciations-leave-lasting-impact-on-individuals/.

17 Mike Fromowitz, "Hall of Shame: More Multicultural Brand Blunders,"
    campaign, February 9, 2017, https://www.campaignasia.com/article/hall-of
    -shame-more-multicultural-brand-blunders/433601.

18 The Opportunity Agenda, "Media Portrayals and Black Male Outcomes," 2011,
    https://opportunityagenda.org/messaging_reports/media-representations-black
    -men-boys/media-portrayals-black-men/.

19 USC Annenberg, "New Study from Annenberg Inclusion Initiative Reveals
    Erasure and Demeaning Portrayal of Muslims Characters Across 200 Top
    Films," June 10, 2021, https://annenberg.usc.edu/news/research-and-impact/new
    -study-annenberg-inclusion-initiative-reveals-erasure-and-demeaning.

20 Patrick Coffee, "LGBT Representation in Ads Has Grown, but Many Consumers
    Find It Inauthentic," *Wall Street Journal*, November 1, 2022, https://www.wsj
    .com/articles/lgbt-representation-in-ads-has-grown-but-many-consumers-find
    -it-inauthentic-11667331187;

21 Kurt Wagner, "This Is How Facebook Collects Data on You Even If You Don't
    Have an Account," Vox.com, April 20, 2018, https://www.vox.com/2018/4/20
    /17254312/facebook-shadow-profiles-data-collection-non-users-mark
    -zuckerberg.

22 Randy Lobasso, "New Black- and Latino-Owned Shop Aims to Expand the Cycling Community,"*GridPhilly*, July 12, 2021, https://gridphilly.com/blog-home /2021/07/12/new-black-and-latino-owned-shop-aims-to-expand-the-cycling -community/.

23 Lobasso, "New Black- and Latino-Owned Shop Aims to Expand the Cycling Community."

24 Peter Walker, "Choice Overload 'Leads to Cart Abandonment,'" *Retail Systems*, May 21, 2019, https://www.retail-systems.com/rs/iAdvize_Survey_Cart _Abandonment_Choice_Overload.php.

25 Kaveh Safavi et al., "U.S. Health Plans Can Save Billions by Helping Patients Navigate the System," *Harvard Business Review*, November 6, 2018, https://hbr .org/2018/11/u-s-health-plans-can-save-billions-by-helping-patients-navigate -the-system.

26 Alina Tugend, "Too Many Choices: A Problem That Can Paralyze," *New York Times*, February 26, 2010, https://www.nytimes.com/2010/02/27/your-money /27shortcuts.html.

27 Stephen J. Dubner, "Should America Be Run by. . . .Trader Joe?," Freaknomics podcast, November 28, 2018, https://freakonomics.com/podcast/should-america -be-run-by-trader-joes/.

28 "About Us," Trader Joe's, https://www.traderjoes.com/home/about-us.

29 Ashley Lutz, "How Trader Joe's Sells Twice as Much as Whole Foods," *Business Insider*, October 7, 2014, https://www.businessinsider.com/trader-joes-sales -strategy-2014-10.

30 Jason Cohen, "It Would Take 17 Hours to Read the Terms & Conditions of the 13 Most Popular Apps," *PCMag*, December 4, 2020, https://www.pcmag.com /news/it-would-take-17-hours-to-read-the-terms-conditions-of-the-13-most -popular.

31 Michael Corkery, "Wells Fargo Fined $185 Million for Fraudulently Opening Accounts," *New York Times*, September 8, 2016, https://www.nytimes.com/2016 /09/09/business/dealbook/wells-fargo-fined-for-years-of-harm-to-customers .html; Office of Public Affairs, US Department of Justice, "Wells Fargo Agrees to Pay $3 Billion to Resolve Criminal and Civil Investigations into Sales Practices Involving the Opening of Millions of Accounts Without Customer Authorization," press release, February 21, 2020, https://www.justice.gov/opa/pr /wells-fargo-agrees-pay-3-billion-resolve-criminal-and-civil-investigations -sales-practices#:~:text=Wells%20Fargo%20%26%20Company%20and%20 its,to%20provide%20millions%20of%20accounts.

32 HelloFresh Terms & Conditions, 10.3 and 10.4 (see https://www.hellofresh.com /about/termsandconditions).

33 HelloFresh, "HelloFresh SE Reaches €7.6bn Revenue for the FY 2022 and Reports over 1bn Meals Shipped to Customers Around the World," press release,

March 7, 2023, https://ir.hellofreshgroup.com/websites/hellofresh/English/3900 /news-detail.html?newsID=2459531.

34 Don Norman, "I Wrote the Book on User-Friendly Design. What I See Today Horrifies Me," *Fast Company,* August 5, 2019, https://www.fastcompany.com/9033 8379/i-wrote-the-book-on-user-friendly-design-what-i-see-today-horrifies-me.

35 Norman, "I Wrote the Book on User-Friendly Design."

36 For more, see the World Central Kitchen website (https://wck.org/relief).

37 "Credit Union Industry Leader, TruStage, Spearheads Strategic Transaction to Propel Fintech Happy Money Forward," *Cision PRNewsWire,* press release, November 15, 2023. https://www.prnewswire.com/news-releases/credit-union -industry-leader-trustage-spearheads-strategic-transaction-to-propel-fintech -happy-money-forward-301988447.html

38 Wein et al., "The Psychology of Consumer Dignity."

39 Tom Wein et al., "Qualitative Experiences of Dignity in the United States: What We Learned About Lives and Cultures of Respect from 4,374 Stories," *IDinsight,* October 5, 2023, https://www.idinsight.org/article/qualitative-experiences-of -dignity-in-the-united-states-what-we-learned-about-lives-and-cultures-of -respect-from-4374-stories/.

40 Tom Wein and Cait Lamberton, "Comparing Experiences of Dignity Cross-Culturally—Evidence from the US, India and Nigeria," *IDinsight,* forthcoming.

Chapter 2

1 Don Norman and Bruce Tognazzini," How Apple Is Giving Design a Bad Name," *Fast Company,* November 10, 2015, https://www.fastcompany.com /3053406/how-apple-is-giving-design-a-bad-name.

2 Chris McQueen, "What Made Apple's 1984 Advert So Successful?," *Medium,* July 14, 2021, https://medium.com/age-of-awareness/what-made-apples-1984 -advert-so-successful-dc5af1b073f3.

3 Nick Noel et al., "Black Consumers: Where to Invest for Equity (a Preview)," McKinsey Global Institute for Black Economic Mobility, December 15, 2021, https://www.mckinsey.com/bem/our-insights/black-consumers-where-to-invest -for-equity-a-preview.

4 Audrey Kemp, "World's Best Ads Ever #63: Axe Hits the Sweet Spot with "Chocolate Man," *The Drum,* June 14, 2022, https://www.thedrum.com/news/2022 /06/14/world-s-best-ads-ever-63-axe-hits-the-sweet-spot-with-chocolate-man.

5 Mark Sweney, "Unilever Vows to Drop Sexist Stereotypes from Its Ads," *The Guardian,* June 22, 2016, https://www.theguardian.com/media/2016/jun/22 /unilever-sexist-stereotypes-ads-sunsilk-dove-lynx.

6 Nafisa Shaheen, "How Axe's Latest Ad Is Shattering Stereotypes," July 3, 2019, exchange4media, https://www.exchange4media.com/advertising-news /shattering-stereotypes-97824.html.

7   Daren Poole, "The Power of Inclusion and Diversity in Advertising," *Kantar*, April 20, 2021, https://www.kantar.com/north-america/inspiration/advertising -media/the-power-of-inclusion-and-diversity-in-advertising.

8   Adam R. Pearson, Jonathon P. Schuldt, Rainer Romero-Canyas, Matthew T. Ballew, and Dylan Larson-Konar, "Diverse Segments of the US Public Underestimate the Environmental Concerns of Minority and Low-Income Americans," *PNAS*, October 29, 2018, https://www.pnas.org/doi/10.1073/pnas .1804698115.

9   Karen Attiah, "Pepsi Shows How America Loves to Erase Black Women," *Washington Post*, April 6, 2017, https://www.washingtonpost.com/blogs/post -partisan/wp/2017/04/06/pepsi-shows-how-america-loves-to-erase-black -women/.

10   Joe Berkowitz, "Heineken Just Put Out the Antidote to That Pepsi Kendall Jenner Ad," *Fast Company*, 26 April, 2017. https://www.fastcompany.com /40412848/heineken-just-put-out-the-antidote-to-that-pepsi-kendall-jenner-ad.

11   Jeff Beer, "Here's How Heineken Made That Awesome Antidote to Pepsi's Kendall Jenner Ad," *Fast Company*, May 5, 2017, https://www.fastcompany.com /40416056/heres-how-heineken-made-that-awesome-antidote-to-pepsis-kendall -jenner-ad.

12   Edelman Report, "Heineken Worlds Apart," https://www.edelman.com/work /heineken-worlds-apart.

13   Dignified Storytelling, "The Dignified Storytelling Handbook," Dubai Cares, December 2021, https://dignifiedstorytelling.com/wp-content/uploads/2021/12 /Dignified-Storytelling-Handbook-English-Dec-2021.pdf.

14   From "The Dignified Storytelling Handbook," https://dignifiedstorytelling.com /wp-content/uploads/2021/12/Dignified-Storytelling-Handbook-English-Dec -2021.pdf, accessed November 28, 2023.

15   Brad Tuttle, "Baby Boomers Like Discounts—Just Not the 'Senior Discount,'" *Time*, July 27, 2012, https://business.time.com/2012/07/27/baby-boomers-like -discounts-just-not-the-senior-discount/.

16   Trabian Shorters and the Skillman Foundation; see more at https://www .skillman.org/blog/the-power-of-asset-framing/.

17   Catherine C. Thomas, Nicholas G. Otis, Justin R. Abraham, Hazel Rose Markus, and Gregory M. Walton, "Toward a Science of Delivering Aid with Dignity: Experimental Evidence and Local Forecasts from Kenya," *PNAS Nexus*, June 24, 2020, https://www.pnas.org/doi/10.1073/pnas.1917046117.

18   David Burrows, "How to Use Ethnography for In-Depth Consumer Insight," *Marketing Week*, May 9, 2014, https://www.marketingweek.com/how-to-use -ethnography-for-in-depth-consumer-insight/.

19   For more, see ANA Educational Foundation, "Race and Ethnicity in Advertising: America in the 20th Century," https://raceandethnicity.org/about.

20 António Guterres, "Our Response to COVID-19 Must Respect the Rights and Dignity of Older People," United Nations statement, May 1, 2020, https://www.un.org/en/coronavirus/our-response-covid-19-must-respect-rights-and-dignity-older-people/.

21 Apoorva Mandavilli, "The C.D.C.'s New Challenge? Grappling with Imperfect Science," *New York Times,* January 17, 2022, https://www.nytimes.com/2022/01/17/health/cdc-omicron-isolation-guidance.html.

22 Amit Bhattacharjee, Jonah Berger, and Geeta Menon, "When Identity Marketing Backfires: Consumer Agency in Identity Expression," *Journal of Consumer Research* 41, no. 2 (April 2014): 294–309, https://doi.org/10.1086/676125.

23 Sapna Maheshwari, "Burger King 'O.K. Google' Ad Doesn't Seem O.K. with Google," *New York Times,* April 12, 2017, https://www.nytimes.com/2017/04/12/business/burger-king-tv-ad-google-home.html.

24 James Wohr, "Ad Blocking: What It Is and Why It Matters to Marketers and Advertisers, " *Insider Intelligence,* October 11, 2023, https://www.insiderintelligence.com/insights/ad-blocking/.

25 Leonhard K. Lades and Liam Delaney, "Nudge FORGOOD," *Behavioural Public Policy,* January 27, 2020, https://www.cambridge.org/core/journals/behavioural-public-policy/article/abs/nudge-forgood/06BC9E9032521954E8325798390A998A.

26 "Health and Human Dignity," Abbott Laboratories corporate website, https://www.abbott.com/lifetothefullest.html.

27 Richard Gray, "How Vulnerable Groups Were Left Behind in Pandemic Response," *Horizon-The EU Research and Innovation Magazine,* June 7, 2021, https://ec.europa.eu/research-and-innovation/en/horizon-magazine/how-vulnerable-groups-were-left-behind-pandemic-response.

28 Elana Herbst, Roberta Michnick Golinkoff, and Kathy Hirsh-Pasek, "Holiday Shopping in Gender-Neutral Toy Aisles? Playing for the Future," Brookings, November 10, 2021, https://www.brookings.edu/articles/holiday-shopping-in-gender-neutral-toy-aisles-playing-for-the-future/.

29 Katherine White and Darren W. Dahl, "To Be or *Not* Be? The Influence of Dissociative Reference Groups on Consumer Preferences," *Journal of Consumer Psychology* 4, no. 4 (2006): 404–14, https://doi.org/10.1207/s15327663jcp1604_11.

30 Frederick F. Wherry, Kristin S. Seefeldt, and Anthony S. Alvarez, *Credit Where It's Due: Rethinking Financial Citizenship,* Russell Sage Foundation, 2019, https://www.russellsage.org/publications/credit-where-its-due.

31 JP Morgan Chase for the *Washington Post,* "Driving the Work of Economic Equity in Underserved Communities," *Washington Post,* 2020, https://www.washingtonpost.com/creativegroup/jpmc/driving-the-work-of-economic-equity-in-underserved-communities/.

32 James Pinchin, "Getting Lost in Hospitals Costs the NHS and Patients," *The Guardian*, March 5, 2015, https://www.theguardian.com/healthcare-network /2015/mar/05/lost-hospitals-costs-nhs-patients-navigation.

33 Sandy Dietrich and Erik Hernandez, "Language Use in the United States: 2019," American Community Survey Reports, August 2022, https://www.census.gov /content/dam/Census/library/publications/2022/acs/acs-50.pdf.

34 See more at https://www.packers.com/community/shareholders.

Chapter 3

1 Hook Agency blog, "Have It Your Way: Burger King Tagline History + Lyrics," 2023, https://hookagency.com/blog/have-it-your-way/.

2 John Crudele, "Burger King's Revamped 'Be Your Way' Slogan Isn't Meaty Enough," *New York Post*, May 21, 2014, https://nypost.com/2014/05/21/burger -kings-revamped-be-your-way-slogan-isnt-meaty-enough/.

3 Statista Research Department, "Revenue of Burger King Worldwide from 2004 to 2022," *Statista*, September 18, 2023, https://www.statista.com/statistics /266462/burger-king-revenue/.

4 Kat Eschner, "The Story of Brownie Wise, the Ingenious Marketer Behind the Tupperware Party," *Smithsonian Magazine*, April 10, 2018, https://www .smithsonianmag.com/smithsonian-institution/story-brownie-wise-ingenious -marketer-behind-tupperware-party-180968658/.

5 Jamie Feldman, "Sephora's Genius Basket System Is an Introvert's Dream Come True," *HuffPost*, November 5, 2019, https://www.huffpost.com/entry/sephora -basket-system_l_5dc19326e4b0615b8a9a00e4.

6 Tom Wein et al., "Qualitative Experiences of Dignity in the United States: What We Learned About Lives and Cultures of Respect from 4,374 Stories," IDinsight, October 5, 2023, https://www.idinsight.org/article/qualitative-experiences-of -dignity-in-the-united-states-what-we-learned-about-lives-and-cultures-of -respect-from-4374-stories/.

7 Wein et al., "Qualitative Experiences of Dignity in the United States."

8 Yahong Zhang, "Virtual Try-on: The Next Big Thing in Luxury Business," Haptic Media, March 4, 2021, https://hapticmedia.com/blog/virtual-try-on/.

9 Tom Wein, Heather Lanthorn, and Torben Fischer, "First Steps Toward Building Respectful Development: Three Experiments on Dignity in Aid in Kenya and the United States," *World Development Perspectives* 29 (March 2023): 100485, https://doi.org/10.1016/j.wdp.2023.100485.

10 See more at https://council.nyc.gov/pb/.

11 Interview with Steven Silverstein by Cait Lamberton, March 3, 2022.

12 Sheena S. Iyengar and Mark R. Lepper, "When Choice Is Demotivating: Can One Desire Too Much of a Good Thing?," *Journal of Personality and Social Psychology* 79, no. 6 (2000): 995–1006, https://doi.org/10.1037/0022-3514.79.6.995.

13 Gaelle Walker, "Store Design: Enter the Decompression Zone," *Convenience Store*, May 28, 2019, https://www.conveniencestore.co.uk/your-business/store -design-enter-the-decompression-zone/593764.article.

14 Mark Wilson, "Walmart's New Re-design Looks a Whole Lot Like Target with One Major Difference," *Fast Company*, January 27, 2022, https://www .fastcompany.com/90716222/exclusive-walmarts-new-redesign-looks-a-lot-like -target-with-one-major-difference.

15 Martha Hostetter and Sarah Klein, "Helping Patients Make Better Treatment Choices with Decision Aids," The Commonwealth Fund, 2023, https://www .commonwealthfund.org/publications/newsletter-article/helping-patients-make -better-treatment-choices-decision-aids.

16 Lindsey Bomnin and Stephanie Gosk, "Surprise Medical Bills Lead to Liens on Homes and Crippling Debt," NBC News, March 19, 2019, https://www.nbcnews .com/health/health-news/surprise-medical-bills-lead-liens-homes-crippling-debt -n984371.

17 For more, see Boston Scientific Watchman, https://www.watchman.com/en-us /home.html.

18 For a definition of the endowment effect, see https://www.behavioraleconomics .com/resources/mini-encyclopedia-of-be/endowment-effect/.

19 Knowledge at Wharton, *The High Cost of Returns: Should Retailers Rethink Their Policies?*, podcast, August 10, 2020, https://knowledge.wharton.upenn.edu /podcast/knowledge-at-wharton-podcast/high-cost-of-returns-should-retailers -rethink-policies/.

20 Amanda Mull, "A Sea Change in Plus-Size Fashion," *The Atlantic*, March 18, 2019, https://www.theatlantic.com/health/archive/2019/03/anthropologie-plus -size-clothing/585103/.

21 See more at https://www.universalstandard.com/pages/about-us#:~:text =How%20can%20we%20bring%20all,we'd%20have%20to%20disagree.

22 Wein et al., "Qualitative Experiences of Dignity in the United States."

23 Wein et al.

24 Jenny G. Olson, Brent McFerran, Andrea C. Morales, and Darren W. Dahl, "Wealth and Welfare: Divergent Moral Reactions to Ethical Consumer Choices," *Journal of Consumer Research* 42 (April 2016): 879–96.

25 Report, "Food Deserts in America: Healthy Foods Scarce in Poor Neighborhoods, Yale Researchers Find," *Yale News*, https://news.yale.edu/ 2008/09/10/healthy-foods-scarce-poor-neighborhoods-yale-researchers -find.

26 Brittney McNamara, "People in Africa Are Using #MyAlwaysExperience Talk About Rashes They Think Were Caused by Always Pads," *Teen Vogue*, October 23, 2019, https://www.teenvogue.com/story/myalwaysexperience-allege -rashes-apparently-caused-by-always-products.

27 Ciku Kimeria, "The Story of How Kenyan Women Are Bringing P&G to Task over the Always 'Burning Pads' Saga," *Quartz*, February 26, 2020, https://qz.com /africa/1807045/kenyan-women-take-pg-to-task-over-always-burning-pads.

Chapter 4

1 Aimee Ortiz, "Peloton Ad Is Criticized as Sexist and Dystopian," *New York Times*, December 03, 2019, https://www.nytimes.com/2019/12/03/business/peloton-bike -ad-stock.html.

2 Ortiz, "Peloton Ad Is Criticized as Sexist and Dystopian."

3 "Peloton Community in Conversation with Sporting Equals: Embracing Equity in Sport," Bloomberg press release, April 3, 2023, https://www.bloomberg.com/press -releases/2023-04-03/peloton-community-in-conversation-with-sporting-equals -embracing-equity-in-sport; Leah Groth, "Peloton's Online Community Is Changing the Fitness Game for Moms," *Glamour*, April 9, 2019, https://www.glamour.com /story/pelotons-online-community-is-changing-the-fitness-game-for-moms.

4 Willem Roper, "Peloton Sales Double During Pandemic," *Statista*, September 8, 2020, https://www.statista.com/chart/22836/peloton-annual-sales/

5 David Curry, "Peloton Revenue and Usage Statistics (2023)," *Business of Apps*, August 1, 2023, https://www.businessofapps.com/data/peloton-statistics/.

6 Lorraine Twohill, "Making Sure Everyone Feels 'Seen on Pixel,'" Google company announcement, February 10, 2022, https://blog.google/inside-google /company-announcements/super-bowl-ad-2022/.

7 Google, "How Real Tone Helps Make a More Equitable Camera," https://store .google.com/intl/en/ideas/articles/inclusive-photography-real-tone/, accessed November 27, 2023.

8 Patrick Holland, "Google Builds Equity into the Pixel 6 with Real Tone Photos and New Voice Features," CNET, October 21, 2021, https://www.cnet.com/tech /mobile/google-builds-equity-into-the-pixel-6-with-real-tone-photos-and-new -voice-features/.

9 Ben Schoon, "Pixel 6 Solidifies Google's Top 5 Slot in North America with Nearly 400% Growth in Q1," *9to5Google*, May 19, 2022, https://9to5google.com /2022/05/19/pixel-6-us-market-q1-2022/.

10 Dilip Soman, "How to Get Consumers to Walk the 'Last Mile'," *The Globe and Mail*, September 8, 2015, https://www.theglobeandmail.com/report-on-business/careers /the-future-of-work/how-to-get-consumers-to-walk-the-last-mile/article26261340.

11 Andrew Limbong, "Can a Patient Gown Makeover Move Hospitals to Embrace Change?," NPR News, February 11, 2018, https://www.ideastream.org/2018-02-11 /can-a-patient-gown-makeover-move-hospitals-to-embrace-change.

12 Bob Tedeschi, "Why Do Hospitals Bare Butts When There Are Better Gowns Around?," *Stat News*, January 25, 2018, https://www.statnews.com/2018/01/25 /hospital-gowns-design/.

13   Henry Ford Health System, "Detroit Designed 'Model G' Has Patients Covered at Henry Ford Hospital," *Cision PR Newswire*, April 16, 2015, https://www.prnewswire.com/news-releases/detroit-designed-model-g-has-patients-covered-at-henry-ford-hospital-300067226.html.

14   Tedeschi, "Why Do Hospitals Bare Butts?"

15   Limbong, "Can a Patient Gown Makeover Move Hospitals to Embrace Change?"

16   Kaitlyn Tiffany, "Period-Tracking Apps Are Not for Women," Vox.com, November 16, 2018, https://www.vox.com/the-goods/2018/11/13/18079458/menstrual-tracking-surveillance-glow-clue-apple-health.

17   CNN Business, "Why Privacy Experts Are Warning Against Using Period-Tracking Apps," CNN, 2023, https://edition.cnn.com/videos/business/2022/05/20/period-pregnancy-app-tracker-data-privacy-roe-wade-hln-mxp-vpx.hln.

18   Conor Stewart, "Assessment of Top Femtech Apps for Data Gathering Policies Worldwide in 2021," *Statista*, July 1, 2022, https://www.statista.com/statistics/1313953/assessment-of-femtech-apps-for-data-gathering/.

19   For more, see https://twitter.com/melancholynsex/status/1548509621152714752?lang=en.

20   Nicolette F. Sheridan et al., "Patients' Engagement in Primary Care: Powerlessness and Compounding Jeopardy: A Qualitative Study," National Library of Medicine, February 2015, https://pubmed.ncbi.nlm.nih.gov/23033910/.

21   Mark Gurman and Matthew Townsend, "How the Apple Store Lost Its Luster," Bloomberg, May 7, 2019, https://www.bloomberg.com/news/articles/2019-05-07/apple-store-locations-reviews-show-customer-service-in-decline#xj4y7vzkg.

22   Zoe Kooyman, "Pumpkins, Markets, and One Bad Apple," Free Software Foundation, October 20, 2021, https://www.fsf.org/blogs/community/pumpkins-markets-and-one-bad-apple.

23   Ben Popken, "Get Ready for 'Frustrating' Tax Season as IRS Battles Historic Backlogs and Staff Shortages," NBC News, January 12, 2022, https://www.nbcnews.com/business/consumer/get-ready-frustrating-tax-season-warns-irs-historic-backlogs-staff-sho-rcna11834.

24   Tom Wein et al., "Qualitative Experiences of Dignity in the United States: What We Learned About Lives and Cultures of Respect from 4,374 Stories," IDinsight, October 5, 2023, https://www.idinsight.org/article/qualitative-experiences-of-dignity-in-the-united-states-what-we-learned-about-lives-and-cultures-of-respect-from-4374-stories/.

25   Wein et al., "Qualitative Experiences of Dignity in the United States."

26   "Small-Town Indian Women Lose Fame, Fun and More After TikTok Ban," Al Jazeera, July 22, 2020, https://www.aljazeera.com/features/2020/7/22/small-town-indian-women-lose-fame-fun-and-more-after-tiktok-ban.

27 Jennifer Nason, "'The Zoom Revolution Empowers Women to Speak Up," *Wall Street Journal*, July 2, 2021, https://www.wsj.com/articles/the-zoom-revolution -empowers-women-to-speak-up-11625260956.

28 Nadya Ellerhorst, "Zoom: The Great Height Equalizer," *UDReview*, January 19, 2021, https://udreview.com/zoom-the-great-height-equalizer/.

29 Alex Ledsom, "McDonald's in Marseille Turned into Food Base to Help Needy," *Forbes*, April 25, 2020, https://www.forbes.com/sites/alexledsom/2020/04/25 /french-locals-requisition-empty-mcdonalds-as-a-food-base-to-help-needy/?sh =21cb55f7636f; Alexis Steinman, "L'Après M: Fast Social Food," *Culinary Backstreets*, April 11, 2023 https://culinarybackstreets.com/cities-category /marseille/2023/lapres-m-fast-social-food/.

30 Chris Arnade, "McDonald's: You Can Sneer, but It's the Glue That Holds Communities Together," *The Guardian*, June 8, 2016, https://www.theguardian .com/business/2016/jun/08/mcdonalds-community-centers-us-physical-social -networks.

31 Marcia Chatelain, *Franchise: The Golden Arches in Black America* (New York: Liveright, 2021), https://wwnorton.com/books/9781631498701.

32 Cari D. Lidgett, "Improving the Patient Experience Through a Commit to Sit Service Excellence Initiative," *Patient Experience Journal* 3, no. 2 (2016): 67–72, https://pxjournal.org/journal/vol3/iss2/11/.

33 Priya Khanchandani, "'Poor Doors' Show That Access Isn't for Everyone in London," *Icon*, October 26, 2019, https://www.iconeye.com/design/poor-doors -london-access-housing.

34 Shelby Welinder, "Opinion: City Has Gone from Allowing 'Poor Doors' to Permitting 'Poor Buildings'," *City Limits*, November 4, 2019, https://citylimits .org/2019/11/04/opinion-city-has-gone-from-allowing-poor-doors-to -permitting-poor-buildings/.

35 Job M. T. Krijnen, David Tannenbaum, and Craig R. Fox. "Choice Architecture 2.0: Behavioral Policy as an Implicit Social Interaction," *Behavioral Science & Policy* 3, no. 2 (2017): 1–18, https://davetannenbaum.github.io/documents /KrijnenTannenbaumFox2018.pdf.

Chapter 5

1 The Coca-Cola Company, "Coca-Cola Reports Fourth Quarter and Full Year Results," press release, February 14, 2023, https://investors.coca-colacompany .com/news-events/press-releases/detail/1076/coca-cola-reports-fourth-quarter -and-full-year-2022-results.

2 Tasneem Kibria, "Coca-Cola: The Essence of Brand Loyalty," *The Business Standard*, June 29, 2020. https://www.tbsnews.net/feature/brands/coca-cola -essence-brand-loyalty-99469.

3 Kibria, "Coca-Cola: The Essence of Brand Loyalty."

4 Statista, "Coca-Cola Brand Awareness, Usage, Popularity, Loyalty, and Buzz Among Soft Drink Drinkers in the United States in 2022," *Statista.com,* https://www.statista.com/forecasts/1352607/coca-cola-soft-drinks-brand-profile -in-the-united-states.

5 Suzanne Kounkel and Melanie Boulden, "Coca-Cola CMO on Building Consumer Loyalty, Trust," Deloitte for the *Wall Street Journal*, March 28, 2022, https://deloitte.wsj.com/articles/coca-cola-cmo-on-building-consumer-loyalty -trust-01648487123.

6 Amy Gallo, "The Value of Keeping the Right Customers," *Harvard Business Review*, October 29, 2014, https://hbr.org/2014/10/the-value-of-keeping-the-right-customers.

7 Finances Online, "70 Customer Retention Statistics for 2023: Loyalty Programs & Strategies," https://financesonline.com/customer-retention-statistics/.

8 David Lazarus, "Column: Canceling Subscriptions Shouldn't Be Like Running an Obstacle Course," *Los Angeles Times*, October 27, 2020, https://www.latimes .com/business/story/2020-10-27/column-canceling-subscriptions.

9 Boone Ashworth, "Hate How Hard It Is to Cancel Subscriptions? The FTC Feels You," *Wired*, March 25, 2023, https://www.wired.com/story/ftc-click-to-cancel -subscriptions/.

10 Mabel Komunda and Aihie Osarenkhoe, "Remedy or Cure for Service Failure? Effects of Service Recovery on Customer Satisfaction and Loyalty," *Business Process Management Journal* 18, no. 1 (February 2012): 82–103, https://www .emerald.com/insight/content/doi/10.1108/14637151211215028/full/html.

11 Ko de Ruyter and Martin G. M. Wetzels, "The Impact of Perceived Listening Behavior in Voice-to-Voice Service Encounters," *Journal of Service Research* 2, no. 3 (February 2000): 276–84, https://doi.org/10.1177/109467050023005.v.

12 Interview with Rafe Mazer by Tom Wein, May 6, 2022.

13 Interview with Rafe Mazer.

14 J. D. Power, " Credit Card Issuers Must Confront Consumers' Mounting Debt, J. D. Power Finds," press release, August 17, 2023, https://www.jdpower.com /business/press-releases/2023-us-credit-card-satisfaction-study.

15 Interview with Rafe Mazer.

16 "US Companies Losing Customers as Consumers Demand More Human Interaction, Accenture Study Finds," press release, March 23, 2016, https:// newsroom.accenture.com/news/2016/us-companies-losing-customers-as -consumers-demand-more-human-interaction-accenture-strategy-study-finds.

17 Laura Stampler, "Recording of Man's Attempt to Cancel Comcast Will Drive You Insane," *Time*, July 15, 2014, https://time.com/2985964/comcast-cancel-ryan-block/.

18 Jordan Weissmann, "A Former Comcast Employee Explains That Horrifying Customer Service Call," *Slate*, July 16, 2014, https://www.slate.com/blogs /moneybox/2014/07/16/comcast_customer_service_an_employee_explains_why _they_won_t_let_you_cancel.html.

19   Tony Hsieh, "How I Did It: Zappos's CEO on Going to Extremes for Customers," *Harvard Business Review*, July–August 2010, https://hbr.org/2010/07/how-i-did -it-zapposs-ceo-on-going-to-extremes-for-customers.

20   Chinedu Okafor, "See Impressive Figures That Demonstrate Kenya's Growth in Its Mobile Market," *Business Insider Africa*, March 9, 2023, https://africa .businessinsider.com/local/markets/see-impressive-figures-that-demonstrate -kenyas-growth-in-its-mobile-market/h728drz

21   Rob Matheson, "Study: Mobile Money Services Lift Kenyans out of Poverty," *MIT News*, December 8, 2016, https://news.mit.edu/2016/mobile-money -kenyans-out-poverty-1208.

22   Tracy Mutinda, "Confusion as Kenyans Receive Contradicting Messages on SIM Registration," *The Star*, April 13, 2022, https://www.the-star.co.ke/news/2022-04 -13-confusion-as-kenyans-receive-contradicting-messages-on-sim-registration/.

23   For more, see https://twitter.com/Safaricom_Care/status/1103419931205476353.

24   Sharon Maombo, "Telkom, Airtel to Access Mpesa's Pay Bill One Year After Till—Safaricom," *The Star*, April 12, 2022, https://www.the-star.co.ke/business /2022-04-12-telkom-airtel-to-access-mpesas-pay-bill-one-year-after-till -safaricom/.

25   See more at https://www.forbes.com/companies/safaricom/?list=world-best -employers&sh=3811166f2ced.

26   Acquah Nana Yeboah, "Kenyan Telco Safaricom Is Facing a $2.38 Billion Lawsuit," *Techloy*, March 8, 2023, https://www.techloy.com/safaricom-faces-2 -38billion-lawsuit/.

27   Alex Fitzpatrick, "Airbnb CEO: 'Bias and Discrimination Have No Place' Here," *Time*, September 8, 2016, https://time.com/4484113/airbnb-ceo-brian-chesky -anti-discrimination-racism/.

28   Ashley Capoot, "Airbnb Beats on Profit and Revenue, Stock Is Up," CNBC, February 14, 2023, https://www.cnbc.com/2023/02/14/airbnb-abnb-earnings-q4 -2022-.html.

Chapter 6

1   Lin-Ling Chiu, Chun-Hao Liu, Chun-Lin Chu, Huang-Li Lin, and Shu-Chung Lii, "Patients' Experiences of Long-Acting Injectable Antipsychotics: A Qualitative Study," *National Library of Medicine*, July 3, 2019, https://www.ncbi .nlm.nih.gov/pmc/articles/PMC6613361/.

Index

About the Authors

Cait Lamberton is the Alberto I. Duran Distinguished Professor of Marketing at the University of Pennsylvania's Wharton School, where she has taught at the undergraduate, MBA, doctoral, and executive levels. Her research focuses on consumer behavior considered both from individual and socially embedded perspectives. In addition to being named a Wharton and Penn fellow, Cait has been designated a Marketing Science Institute Scholar and received the Erin Anderson Award for the field's top female researcher and mentor; the Lazaridis Prize for her research related to technology; and the Hunt/Maynard Award for her conceptual contributions to the field of Marketing. Outside academia, Cait has been retained as a consultant by the US Departments of Labor and Education, as well as pharmaceutical and financial services firms. She holds a BA in English literature from Wheaton College in Wheaton, Illinois; an MBA and PhD from the University of South Carolina; and an honorary doctorate from the University of Lucerne, Switzerland.

Neela A. Saldanha is the executive director at the Yale Research Initiative on Innovation and Scale (Y-RISE) and a behavioral scientist. Previously, she was the founding director for the Centre for Social and Behaviour Change at Ashoka University India, funded by the Bill and Melinda Gates Foundation. Prior to her career in global health and development, Neela spent more than fifteen years in the private sector leading teams in brands, sales, consumer insights, and strategy at Nestlé, Unilever, PepsiCo, and Accenture. Neela has been mentioned in *Forbes* magazine as "Ten Behavioral Scientists You Should Know." Her writing has appeared in *Harvard Business Review*,

Nature Human Behaviour, and *Behavioral Scientist*, among others. She is a board member of The Life You Can Save, founded by the leading philosopher Peter Singer, Grameen Foundation USA, and Her Move Next that encourages girls to stay in chess, among others. She has a PhD in marketing from the Wharton School, University of Pennsylvania; and an MBA from IIM Calcutta, India. Neela lives in New York City with her husband, Tanuj; daughter, Aliya; and gently stubborn cat, Ginger.

Tom Wein is a director at IDinsight. He leads the Dignity Initiative there, building on research he has been doing since 2017. Tom has spent the past thirteen years leading research in the Global South. He has given evidence to the UK Parliament and written several academic papers. He previously led the work of Raising Voices to prevent violence against children in schools in Uganda. Before that, he worked with the Busara Center for Behavioral Economics, where he built the Culture, Research Ethics and Methods (CREME) agenda and led work on activism, civil society and edutainment. Tom holds a master's degree in communication for development from Malmö University in Sweden; and an undergraduate degree in war studies from King's College, London. He works to advance justice and create better governance through useful research, and he believes that research is most useful when it grapples with questions of power. He lives in Nairobi, Kenya, with his wife, Rachel; son, Oliver; and dog, Bailey.

WHARTON
SCHOOL
PRESS

About Wharton School Press

Wharton School Press, the book publishing arm of the Wharton School of the University of Pennsylvania, was established to inspire bold, insightful thinking within the global business community.

An imprint of University of Pennsylvania Press, Wharton School Press publishes a select list of award-winning, bestselling, and thought-leading books that offer trusted business knowledge to help leaders at all levels meet the challenges of today and the opportunities of tomorrow. Led by a spirit of innovation and experimentation, Wharton School Press leverages groundbreaking digital technologies and has pioneered a fast-reading business book format that fits readers' busy lives, allowing them to swiftly emerge with the tools and information needed to make an impact. Wharton School Press books offer guidance and inspiration on a variety of topics, including leadership, management, strategy, innovation, entrepreneurship, finance, marketing, social impact, public policy, and more.

To find books that will inspire and empower you to increase your impact and expand your personal and professional horizons, visit wsp.wharton.upenn.edu.

About the Wharton School

Founded in 1881 as the world's first collegiate business school, the Wharton School of the University of Pennsylvania is shaping the future of business by incubating ideas, driving insights, and creating leaders who change the world. With a faculty of more than 235 renowned professors, Wharton has 5,000 undergraduate, MBA, executive MBA, and doctoral students. Each year, 13,000 professionals from around the world advance their careers through Wharton Executive Education's individual, company-customized, and online programs. More than 100,000 Wharton alumni form a powerful global network of leaders who transform business every day.

www.wharton.upenn.edu

UNIVERSITY OF
PENNSYLVANIA
PRESS

About Penn Press

True to its Philadelphia roots, Penn Press is well known for its distinguished list of publications in American history and culture, including innovative work on the transnational currents that surrounded and shaped the republic from the colonial period through the present, as well as prize-winning publications in urban studies. The Press is equally renowned for its publications in European history, literature, and culture from late antiquity through the early modern period. Penn Press's social science publications tackle contemporary political issues of concern to a broad readership of citizens and scholars, notably including a long-standing commitment to publishing pathbreaking work in international human rights. Penn Press also publishes outstanding works in archaeology, economic history, business, and Jewish studies in partnership with local institutions.

You can learn more about our recent publications by visiting www.pennpress.org or viewing our seasonal catalogs.